Robert Half's Success Guide for Accountants

Second Edition

Robert Half
Robert Half International Inc.

PRENTICE HALL
Englewood Cliffs, New Jersey 07632

Prentice-Hall International (UK) Limited, *London*
Prentice-Hall of Australia Pty. Limited, *Sydney*
Prentice-Hall Canada, Inc., *Toronto*
Prentice-Hall Hispanoamericana, S.A., *Mexico*
Prentice-Hall of India Private Limited, *New Delhi*
Prentice-Hall of Japan, Inc., *Tokyo*
Simon & Schuster Asia Pte. Ltd., *Singapore*
Editora Prentice-Hall do Brasil, Ltda., *Rio de Janeiro*

10 9 8 7 6 5 4

Library of Congress Cataloging-in-Publication Data
Half, Robert.
  Robert Half's success guide for accountants.

  (Accounting and finance practice series)
  Includes index.
  1. Accounting—Vocational guidance. I. Title.
II. Title: Success guide for accountants. III. Series.
HF5657.H34   1987   657'.023'73   87-16430
ISBN 0-13-781535-2

ISBN 0-13-781535-2

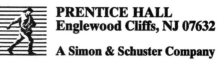

PRENTICE HALL
Englewood Cliffs, NJ 07632

A Simon & Schuster Company

Printed in the United States of America

Contents

Preface

Success has to start somewhere.
Failure needs no beginning.

As an accountant, you do not need to be told that the accounting profession has been changing dramatically over the past two decades and that these changes have opened up extraordinary career opportunities. It's true, of course, that accounting has always been a basic tool in business, but a number of factors—increased government requirements, frequently changing tax legislation, the information revolution, to name just three—have greatly enhanced the role that accountants now play in business. It's hardly a coincidence that today more chief executive officers than ever before are coming out of accounting or financial backgrounds.

If the profession has been changing dramatically, so, too, have the criteria for career success in accounting. The biggest change is simply this: if you aspire to the upper levels of public or management accounting, you can no longer build your career path around technical competence alone. It's not enough, in other words, to be a good "numbers" person. Just as important (if not more important) are skills that have less to do with accounting per se and more to do with your general business acumen and your effectiveness as a person.

Which brings me to this book.

Its purpose is not to make you a "better accountant" in the strict sense of the phrase. Its purpose instead is to show you how you can take the accounting skills you already have and parlay these skills into greater career success.

The advice you'll be receiving in this book is based, in part, on the more than 35 years that I myself have been involved in the career aspects of accounting. But to assure the relevance and the value of the material, I took two additional steps. First, I commissioned Burke Marketing Research to conduct a survey exclusively for this book. The purpose of the survey was to gain insight into the career aspects of accounting from the people in the best position to offer this insight: from managing partners, top management, and personnel directors. Second, I interviewed personally some two dozen of the most successful accountants and executives in North America and I incorporated their observations on career success in accounting into each of the chapters in this book.

The findings that turned up in our survey and in the observations that came out of the interviews should be of interest to every accountant who aspires to a greater degree of career success. They constitute, all in all, important, timely, and highly practical advice on how to manage the most important aspect of your accounting career: yourself.

Robert Half

Acknowledgments

**No one has ever achieved
anything without help.**

In a sense, nearly every accountant I have worked with over the past 35 years has contributed in one way or another to this book, but there are certain people to whom I owe a special debt of gratitude. Many of these people are highly successful accountants and business people who, busy as they are, allowed me to interview them and in their answers to my questions provided much of the insightful advice that appears throughout the book. Their names, as well as the names of others who were instrumental in this project, are: William Aiken, Bob L. Anderson, Kenneth S. Asch, Nancy P. Asch, Isaac Assael, Norman E. Auerbach, Colin Ayley, Frank Bartl, Bonnie Binkert, Dr. Abraham J. Briloff, Dr. James Bulloch, Michael Burgio, Philip B. Chenok, Alex Cohen, Frank M. Davidson, Malcolm S. Forbes, A. Bernard Frechtman, Patricia Frechtman, Alvin M. Galland, Larry Gipple, Harry A. Gilbert, Michael Goldstein, Viola Gouty, A. S. Grishman, Maxine E. Half, Richard S. Hickok, Thomas Hurst, William S. Kanaga, Edward O. Lutz, Buddy Martin, Kenneth Majcen, Eli Mason, Robert Maynard, Robert McCall, Harold M. Messmer, Jr., William J. Morgan, Thomas Murphy, Herbert J. Myers, Caryn Newman, David Newman, Denis J. O'Leary, Dennis A. Osterdock, Robert A. Palmer, Dr. Emanuel Saxe, Debra Scott, Barbara J. Shildneck, Robert Shultis, Marc J. Silbert, Peggy L. Silbert, Saul S. Silverman, Peter Skomorowsky, Patrick L. Southerland,

Charles L. Squires, Barry Tarshis, Sanford Teller, Milton Weinick, William F. Wernersback, Charles J. Wolff, and John Woodcock.

Accounting: A Good Place to Be

1

Accounting for your future is
your most important
accounting function.

A young man I know recently took a job in the sales division of a well-known electronics company. There would be nothing unusual about someone taking such a job, except that this particular young man is a trained accountant who, in fact, had been working for the preceding four years in the company's internal auditing department.

Why the change? "I didn't think I was getting anywhere," he explained to me, and then went on to point out that he was unhappy with the salary he was earning as an auditor, that he was not deriving any feeling of accomplishment from his position, and that he did not feel he was getting enough respect for the work he was doing. He also complained that the accountants in his company were considered "overhead," and that the "real producers" were thought to be in sales. "I was getting more and more frustrated," he said. "I had the feeling that nobody in the company recognized what I was doing. So, when a job opened up in sales, I asked for it and got it."

As it happens, the accountant I just described is anything but a rarity. Accounting, like other professions, is not without its share of professionals who are frustrated and discontented. Numerous surveys published over the past several years indicate that accountants, as a group, are dissatisfied with *many* elements of their jobs, in particular their salaries, their lack of recognition, and their working conditions.

1

Some surveys show that the aspects of their work with which accountants express either a "lack of satisfaction" or "complete dissatisfaction" actually *outnumber* the areas in which they say they are satisfied. These figures hardly add up to a profession overflowing with contentment.

So, you really cannot blame somebody like the young man I am talking about here for giving up on accounting as a career. It may well be that many of you reading this book either have contemplated or are now contemplating a similar move, even though you may be an excellent accountant with many years of experience. Chances are, too, that the work itself is not at the root of your dissatisfaction (most accountants, according to surveys taken on the subject, enjoy the actual work). It is more than likely the situation in your firm, your department, or your practice.

You may feel, for instance, that you are not making the money you should be making compared with how hard you have to work and how much you contribute to your company or to the clients you serve. You may know business people, lawyers, or consultants who are further along in their careers than you, even though you believe you are more intelligent and have a better knowledge of business in general. Perhaps you are working for a CPA firm that, in your view, does not give enough responsibility or the chance to make important decisions. You may be a management accountant in a large company that, as you see it, does not attach enough value to your work or, for that matter, the work of your entire department. You may be beginning to wonder if you made a mistake by becoming an accountant in the first place. Perhaps you have come to the conclusion, as one disgruntled accountant I know once said, that "The only way to get ahead in accounting is to get out of it."

As one whose specialty for more than 35 years has been filling accounting and other financial positions, I can certainly understand and sympathize with these sentiments. I would also be the last person to suggest that the complaints accountants are voicing today are totally unjustified. In my view, many accountants do *not* command either the salaries or the respect they deserve, considering the services they provide. Unfortunately, too, many corporations today do see accountants as overhead rather than producers.

Yet, in spite of these conditions, in spite of the gap between what accountants do and what some accountants receive by way of money and recognition, the last thing I would ever recommend to an accountant today is to *abandon* the profession, especially now. I will go even further. If anything, accounting may well be today's *best* route to a successful business career—so much so that if I myself were a young man or young woman starting in college today, accounting would again be my major field of study.

I base this bullish outlook on a number of factors. First of all, unlike many other professions today, (law and teaching, for example), the demand for accountants appears to be growing, and not shrinking, though the growth rate is not as pronounced as it was in the late 1960s and early 1970s. *Forbes* magazine, while noting that graduates with accounting degrees will rise from 59,000 in 1981 to 70,000 in 1985, has maintained nonetheless that "demand will outstrip supply." A survey by the American Institute of Certified Public Accountants (AICPA) indicated a 7 per cent growth rate in demand for public accountants throughout the rest of the decade.

These encouraging statistics, moreover, are backed up the findings of several surveys, included one conducted by Burke Marketing Research expressly for this book. The respondents in this survey were CPA partners, chief financial officers, top management personnel, and personnel directors from the nation's largest companies; I will be referring to specific findings throughout the book. One finding, however, deserves mention right here: 90 per cent of the respondents in the survey felt that opportunities in today's business climate were "better than ever" for accountants. This finding was reinforced by a study by the National Association of Accountants, which found that 90 per cent of top management felt that accounting will be come more critical to decision makers in the years ahead. The results of both these surveys are borne out by the views of virtually all the accountants and business executives I interviewed for this book. As Malcolm S. Forbes, Chairman of *Forbes* magazine, told me, "Things are going to be more complicated in business, not less, and this means that accountants are going be in more demand."

Other reasons that go beyond statistics support the view that accounting is an excellent field to be in these days. The recession in the early 1980s, for one thing, has produced a dramatic shift in corporate priorities, with the result that major corporations are far more concerned than ever before with financial planning and are relying more and more on their own financial personnel and on their public accounting firms to help them make key decisions.

At the same time, a number of factors—the recent overhauling of the federal tax code, the proliferating number of financing devices, and the ever-increasing reporting and auditing requirements placed on American businesses by the IRS, the SEC, the FTC, and the rest of the government alphabet—have given added stature and power to their accounting departments. When I started my first job in accounting, many years ago, the business of business was a lot simpler. If a company wanted to raise money, it simply borrowed from its bank or issued common or preferred stock or bonds and did not consider devices like convertible bonds, leasing, floating rate preferred shares, and interest rate swaps. Years ago, when the time came to evaluate a company's assets, one simply looked at inventories, buildings, and equipment, and never gave any thought to many of the intangibles—research capabilities, for example—that have now become part of the asset evaluation process. Even more financial sophistication is needed to plan and manage pension funds and to set up compensation packages.

No wonder, then, that we are seeing more and more corporations choosing as their chief executive officers managers with accounting and finance backgrounds. According to a *Fortune Magazine* survey, nearly 25 per cent of the 800 highest paid CEOs in the United States have financial backgrounds.

So, the opportunities in accounting are *there*—and they are growing. The opportunities are particularly good these days for women. Accounting, in fact, may well offer women the best overall route for moving ahead quickly. Admittedly, men on the partnership levels in CPA firms still outnumber women by a substantial margin, but, as more and more women enter the profession, it is only a matter of time until the proportion of women partners grows. Women *are* entering the profession in unprecedented numbers. Arthur Young reported that 40 per cent of its new professional employees are women and that women account for nearly a third of its managerial staff. Not surprisingly, a recent study of future trends published by the Colorado Society of CPAs predicted that, by the early 1990s, more than one-third of the partners in CPA firms will be women. The publication *Boardroom Reports* went so far as to assert that, in 10 years, "more than half of the new-partner admissions" in the largest public accounting firms would be women. The *Boardroom Reports* rationale, based on the views of a current partner with a major CPA firm, is this: "It is generally accepted that the best business students today are women."

Meanwhile, the most recent surveys show that some 40 per cent of college graduates with accounting degrees are women, and that women represent nearly a third of the young recruits in the larger firms. A survey my company did showed that when a man and a woman competed for the same accounting job (the jobs paid between $15,000 and $50,000), a woman got the job 72 per cent of the time. "The good news for women in accounting," says a woman editor in the accounting field, "is that they're no longer perceived as full-charge bookkeepers but as accountants. Women are more visible than ever before in the profession, and the top firms are going out of their way to hire them."

HOW THE PROFESSION IS CHANGING

At the root of these broadened opportunities in accounting are a number of dramatic changes that have occurred in the profession over the past quarter-century—changes you surely know about. Gone are the days, for instance, when the major public accounting firms confined their activities to pure accounting and based their practices almost entirely on auditing. Today, it is the rare medium-sized or larger public accounting firm that does not have its own tax and management advisory services (MAS) department, relying more and more on fees from these services. Not long ago, Arthur Andersen reported that its fees from consulting services were up 30 per cent from the previous year and were the prime contributor to a 21 per cent increase in overall fees. Interestingly, too, while accounting and auditing represented 61 per cent of Andersen's chargeable hours, these two services accounted for only 54 per cent of its revenue. The reason: the average fee per hour for auditing is less than for tax and consulting.

Gone, too, are the days when CPA firms were loathe to advertise their services or to compete directly with one another for major accounts. What is happening in accounting is similar to what has happened, to a great extent, in the investment industry, in banking, and in law. The traditional, leisurely—some would call it "gentlemanly"—way of doing business has given way to a more aggressive, more openly competitive business style. Accounting firms today are relying more and more on advertising agencies and, in some instances, public relations firms, and you hear much more talk than you used to in these companies about "marketing." Symbolizing the change has been a noticeable increase in allegations that some of the larger public accounting firms engage in "low balling" (underbidding) in order to get new clients—a practice that was unheard of as recently as 15 years ago.

The changes I have just mentioned were chronicled not long ago by a *Chicago Sun Times* reporter named Mark Brown, who noted, among other things, that Coopers & Lybrand had engaged the firm of New Dimensions Marketing to do its public relations, and that Deloitte Haskins & Sells, in the spring of 1979, became the first international public accounting firm to embark on a major advertising campaign. Brown also made note of the decision of Alexander Grant (Grant Thornton) in 1982 to hold a press conference on the new federal tax legislation two weeks before President Reagan signed the bill. "While the competition was snarling at their audacity," wrote Brown, "Alexander Grant basked in two weeks of press clippings." Brown added: "That kind of clawing might not be unusual in most of the business world, but it is for most accounting firms, many of whom still hang on their to their old euphemism for marketing—'practice development' or PD."

Not everyone in accounting, of course, is pleased with the direction the profession has taken over the past few years. Some people, for instance, believe that the increasing involvement in MAS, not to mention the increase in executive recruiting activity among some CPA firms, represents an inherent conflict of interest. How can you maintain your independence, some people want to know, when the client you are auditing is also an MAS client or has key personnel that you recruited?

Also, not everyone is pleased that the profession has become so competitive that the power in many firms lies not with the most skilled accountants, but with accountants who can bring in the most business. Increased competition among the big CPA firms, noted Englishman, Anthony Hilton, in an article that appeared in the June 1982 issue of *Management Accounting*, has become an "undignified scramble—a quite open effort to steal clients." This view is shared by more than a few American accountants.

In any case, the trend toward a more competitive, broader-based profession is well entrenched, so well entrenched that in some of the larger firms, MAS services now account for as much as 15 per cent of yearly revenues. No one is surprised anymore when, say, Coopers & Lybrand is hired by Sun Oil Company to set up an inventory system for Sun's gasoline products, or by American Can to improve cash management. No one is surprised when Arthur Andersen is hired by a large waste disposal company in Chicago to design an information system for its chemical division, or when Price Waterhouse is hired by the United States Postal Service to design and put into operation a payroll system capable of processing checks for 700,000 postal workers.

What it all means, then, is that while career prospects for accountants have never been better, there are new demands on accountants who hope to become more successful. It is one thing to be in demand, and something else again to *meet* that demand, and most people who are in the thick of this new surge of accounting activity in business would agree that many firms are finding it difficult to keep pace with the intensified demand for their services. "The problem isn't so much technical competence," says the managing partner of a very successful

Midwestern accounting firm. "It's more the fact that many of our accountants now find themselves in situations they've never encountered before. Our accountants have much more direct client contact than ever before. They have to give presentations. They have to inspire confidence. And a lot of them don't know how to do it."

Few would argue the point: it is no longer enough in accounting to be a competent or even better than competent technician—not if your ambition is to reach the upper echelons of the profession. With rare exceptions, the accountants today who are moving ahead quickly these days are men and women whose skills go well beyond the basic tools of the trade. They are good business people, good managers, good communicators, and, in many cases, good "sales people." "They are men and women who," in the words of Donald C. Agnew, southwestern managing partner for the CPA firm of KMG Main Hurdman (Peat Marwick Main & Co.) "are able to translate accounting knowledge into business knowledge and are able to channel their capacity for leadership into productive results." Or, as Malcolm Forbes says, "What is really in high demand in accounting is intelligence—the ability to not only produce the numbers but to dig out the meaning of them. An intelligent accountant has an unlimited future."

Virtually all the professionals I interviewed for this book expressed the same basic viewpoint as Malcolm Forbes and Donald Agnew, that is, to get ahead today in accounting, you need to be more than an "accountant" in the traditional sense of the term. William Morgan, a CPA with Peat Marwick, stresses, for instance, that accountants who want to get ahead in the profession must have certain personality traits that were not as critical 20 years ago. "The need today," he says, "is for individuals who are aggressive, inquisitive and highly motivated." Patrick Lamkin Southerland, a CPA who heads the Robert Half Washington, D.C., franchise, points out that the higher you move up the ladder in accounting, the more important nonaccounting skills become. "Particularly," says Southerland, "the ability to interact with people throughout the company—the ability to not only analyze what it is happening throughout a company, but to present to the company in a politically astute way."

Alvin A. Galland, a CPA who is the chief financial officer of Robert Half International Inc., believes that, more than ever before, an accountant today must be a generalist: "someone who can take financial information and apply it to a variety of issues." Michael Goldstein, national managing partner of professional services with Laventhol & Horwath, stresses the selling aspect of accounting today. "The accountant in the past," he says, "was able to go off into a corner to work and work and would still be able to keep clients. No more. The field today is much more competitive and selling is a major part of what you have to do to succeed."

What all these people are saying, in short, is that the era of the "green shade" accountant is well behind us. If you want to get ahead in accounting today, your must recognize that being technically proficient is only half the battle. The rest has to do with the ability to advise, to manage, and to play a direct role in a company's growth.

WHAT THIS BOOK WILL DO FOR YOU

It is not the purpose of this book to make you a "better" accountant per se. I am assuming that you understand your profession and that you are a solid technician. I am not going to try to increase your knowledge of tax law, make you a better auditor, or improve your financial planning skills. Instead, I will focus on skills that relate purely to *career* success in today's business climate: to the things you should know and to the things you should be doing to *use* the skills and knowledge you have developed in school and in your professional experience to further your career goals, regardless of whether these goals lie within the accounting profession itself or in the corporate world as a whole.

What will concern us in this book is not so much how "good" an accountant you are, but how effectively you are now structuring and managing your career; how you handle yourself on the job; how you deal with the people you work for and work with; how you communicate, delegate, and manage; and how you market and promote yourself or your firm, in other words, how you do all the things that, as you will see, are as instrumental to your success as your technical knowledge and skills.

My premise for getting ahead in accounting is a simple one: to generate the highest level of career success out of your accounting background and knowledge, your level of expertise must extend *beyond* the balance sheet and the profit and loss statement. To reach these levels, you have to think of yourself as a business person *first*, and as an accountant second.

Do not misunderstand me. I am not downplaying the importance of technical skills and knowledge, nor do I contend that business acumen and managerial expertise are more important than the basic disciplines of this profession. As I indicated earlier, the demand for accountants is growing, but the critical shortage in accounting today is not so much among technicians but among accountants who can think and perform beyond the normal spheres of accounting. The shortage is of accountants who can manage effectively, communicate effectively—in short, function more as executives and business people than as financial specialists.

What are the skills that underlie these functions? How do they relate to accounting? How do you develop them? These are just some of the questions we will be looking into. The answers you will be receiving come from a variety of sources: from surveys and studies, from interviews with people who have parleyed their knowledge of accounting into highly successful business careers, and from my own experience as the founder and head of the largest recruiting company in the world that specializes in accounting financial personnel.

Above all, I want to prove to you that there is no great mystery to becoming successful in accounting and that people at the top of the profession today are there because they knew how to get there and were not simply lucky enough to be in the right place at the right time.

I have come to know one accountant very well over the years, a man I will call Fred. I mention Fred because he is highly successful today—the president of a corporation that manufactures electrical components. Yet, not very long ago at all, Fred considered himself a failure as an accountant. When I first met Fred about twelve years ago, he had been through four different jobs in less than six years, and he was so disenchanted with accounting, that he was thinking of getting out of it. "I'm just not a good numbers person," he insisted. "I don't really belong in accounting."

True, Fred was *not* a particularly good numbers person. But he had other skills. He was a good manager. He got along well with people. He knew how to plan and coordinate long-term projects. He was much better, in other words, with people than he was with numbers.

Fred had some interesting choices to make. He could have abandoned accounting altogether and moved into some other area—marketing, for instance. But he did not. Instead, he applied for—and got—an accounting position in which the major part of his job was supervising other accountants. He flourished. He was promoted to controller, then treasurer, and, ultimately, president of the firm.

I grant you, success stories like the story I have just told you are not everyday occurrences. But, the lesson of Fred's story is one that all accountants might well take to heart. Some people might contend that Fred was simply "lucky" to land a job in a company that suited his particular skills. But, I have always believed that the "luckiest" people are the people who work the hardest at being lucky. I agree, Fred was fortunate to find a job that would eventually lead to a presidency. It was not luck that he did so well in the job he took, nor was it luck that led him to seek the top job he eventually got.

What happened to Fred—the success he achieved—can happen to you and it can happen in any number of different ways: as a partner in a CPA firm, as the controller or president of a company, as a successful practitioner on your own, or in countless business situations in which you use your accounting background. "The horizons account-ants have today are so exciting," says Saul S. Silverman, a successful CPA and attorney, "that anyone with a good level of competitive desire to serve *must* be successful." Yes, you can go far in accounting, farther than you may think. I am going to do my best in this book to point you in the right direction.

Do You Really Want to Be Successful?

2

The easy way to success is to work hard.

Vic Braden, the well-known tennis coach and television personality, often talks about a conversation he once overheard between a tournament promoter and the tennis champion Jimmy Connors. The tournament director was trying to interest Connors in his tournament, and Connors wanted to know about the prize money.

"Well," said the tournament director. "If you come in first, you win $30,000. And if you come in second . . ."

He never got a chance to finish the sentence. Said Connors, "I'm not interested in second place."

Indeed he was not. The fact is, if you talk to highly successful people in any field, from tennis to accounting, you will find substantially the same attitude: no special interest in second place. In fact, of all the attributes that characterize highly successful people in general and highly successful accountants in particular, none is more universal than the simple *desire* to succeed. As Richard S. Hickock, CPA, former Chairman of Main Hurdman (now Peat Marwick Main & Co.) likes to put it, "The one thing nearly all successful accountants have in common is that they are not satisfied with the success they currently enjoy."

I am not suggesting here that, to be successful in accounting, the only thing you really need is a great *desire* to be successful—hardly. Accounting, after all, is a complex and demanding field and if you lack

11

the intelligence, the judgment, the technical skills, and the discipline this complexity requires, you are not going to get very far, regardless of how ambitious you are. A lot of tennis players, remember, have as much competitive desire as Jimmy Connors had, but not too many of them could hit the backhand as hard.

On the other hand, what is lacking in most of the accountants I have met over the past 35 years is not technical skills or intelligence, but the ability—and, in many cases, the desire—to direct these technical skills to a predetermined goal. What is lacking is a true commitment to success.

Let me point out here that, by "commitment to success," I do not mean that you need to be *compulsively* driven to succeed—driven to the point that you ignore everything else in your life, in particular, your family. To the contrary, as Charles A. Garfield, a California psychologist who has studied hundreds of top performers in business and other fields, points out, "optimal performers" are not, as a rule, workaholics or the so-called Type A behavior personality. They take vacations, they enjoy close family relationships, they know when to stop working, and they are good at managing their stress.

But, regardless of your capabilities, you cannot take success for granted. You have to *want* it and you have to go after it. Milton Weinick, CPA, a partner of a very successful public accounting firm, Weinick, Sanders & Co., said, "You not only have to want success, you have to give your bosses and your clients what *they* want." Weinick then added, "The mistake so many people make is they believe that all people have the same requirements, and they therefore give them all the same service. It's important to determine what various people want, and then customize your service to satisfy each of them. Those that do that have a leg up on the ladder of success."

You need what I like to think of as a "healthy" appetite for success (however you choose to define it) as an important goal for yourself, and you have to organize a good portion of your life toward that goal.

"Nearly all of the successful accountants I know," says Professor Edward O. Lutz, a CPA who is the director of accounting programs at Brooklyn College, "are success-oriented in one way or another. They have their own success goals. In some cases, it may be to become the best technician. In other cases, it might be to become the managing partner of a major CPA firm. Whatever it is, they are *aiming* for something."

It is worth pointing out that Edward Lutz's own success goals underwent a dramatic change in the middle of his career. For 20 years, starting in the late 1940s, he was both an instructor at Brooklyn College and a partner in his own accounting practice. He says,

> The only trouble is that I was working 80 hours a week and my wife didn't want to be a rich young widow. So, I opted to get out of my accounting business and teach. I wanted to reduce my obligations, live longer, and I decided there was no point in storing up more money. I wanted to enjoy life. Analyzing both of my careers, I decided to give up the deadlines and the pressures of public accounting and continue being just a college professor.

Lutz's career is instructive to think about for a couple of reasons. First of all, it underscores the fact that success does not come without hard work. Secondly, it illustrates the fact that success is a relative concept. Lutz, like many successful accountants, reached a stage in his career where he felt fulfilled. Had he been a different person, he might have reached this point much earlier or much later. The key point to bear in mind, however, is that Lutz made this decision himself: it was not made for him.

I am not maintaining that the only way to become successful is to work 80 hours a week. I recognize the crucial difference between being committed to success and being a workaholic, "someone who has nothing else in his or her life *except* work." Even so, it is important to recognize that success is not a game you can play now and then when the spirit moves you. You have to play the game on a constant basis, which is to say that the part of the mind concerned with success should be "on call" at all times.

When you take a vacation, for instance, I would be the last person to tell you to bring work with you. Then again, if, while you are on vacation, you meet someone who might be helpful to your career, you would be foolish not to establish contact and make arrangements to meet when the two of you are back at work.

Here is another example. I enjoy what I think is an active leisure life. I travel. I play golf. I read. But, whatever I am doing, I always have a small notebook and pen—or often, a mini-tape recorder—with me. That way, if an idea should occur to me, I can write it down or record it immediately. In fact, I developed many of the thoughts for this book while walking or driving. I would suggest that you keep a pad and pen (one of those pens that have a built-in light), or a recorder, on the night table beside your bed. You never know when you might wake up in the middle of the night with an idea or a solution to a problem you have been trying to solve all day.

These are little things, I grant you, and you may think of them as inconsequential. The point, though, is that success is often nothing more than the combined effect of a number of "inconsequentials." Think about it a minute. Think about how much more productive you could be if you could train your mind to function 24 hours a day, not to be consumed with work 24 hours of day, but to be receptive at any time during the day to any idea or person who could be helpful in your career.

SUCCESS PATTERNS IN ACCOUNTING

Over the past several years, there have been a number of studies on the traits that make people successful. No study I know of has been done specifically on accountants, but I have developed my own ideas on the subject, based on interviews with some of the most successful people in the field. As far as I have been able to tell, most of the people at the top of the accounting profession share the following traits:

They view getting ahead as a goal unto itself

They work very hard

They are not afraid to put themselves on the line

They have a great deal of intellectual curiosity

They like what they do and are guided by "internal" goals of excellence

I am not saying that these are the *only* traits successful accountants share, but these are the traits that have continually emerged in the many conversations I have had with leading accountants. So, let us look at each a little more closely.

GETTING AHEAD AS A GOAL UNTO ITSELF

Norman E. Auerbach is a CPA and attorney who, for many years, was the chairman of Coopers & Lybrand. He began his professional accounting career in 1947 in the firm which eventually became Coopers & Lybrand—a firm then known as Lybrand, Ross Bros. & Montgomery. William Aiken is a CPA and partner in Peat Marwick Main & Co. and a past president of the National Association of Black Accountants. He began his career as a clerk typist and then joined the Marines so that he could take advantage of the GI bill and attend college at night.

Here we have two accountants with two entirely different career paths, yet sharing one thing in common: a driving desire to move up the success ladder.

Norman Auerbach is interesting not only for what he did while he was *in* accounting but for what he planned to do when he would retire at the age of 62. In the early 1950s, while he was moving up the ranks at his firm, Auerbach went to school at night at St. John's University to earn a law degree and was admitted to bar in 1955. But, he never had a chance to practice law until he retired his chairmanship at Coopers & Lybrand, and accepted an offer to associate himself with a law firm. "This is something that as a young man I always wanted to do," he explains. "Only it's happening a 'few years' later."

William Aiken, unlike Auerbach, worked for a number of different organizations after getting into accounting. His first accounting job was as a senior accounting clerk. He then became a state insurance examiner, spent some time with Arthur Young, partnered his own firm for a while, and then went to work in New York City as Deputy Commissioner of Human Resources, before assuming his present affiliation.

The steady rise of these two men typifies a pattern you will find among most accountants who have achieved a high level of success. But this pattern happens to differ dramatically from the pattern that typifies most accountants—that of finding a comfortable niche and staying there. "One of the main things that holds accountants back today," says Richard Hickock, "is that people become satisfied with whatever level they're on and don't feel the need to move upward."

There is nothing *wrong*, of course, with being so satisfied with your present job that you are not really interested in bettering your position. If you are happy in your present situation, I do not want to stir up discontentment. The question you need to ask yourself, however, is whether your satisfaction is genuine or whether it is simply a reflection of your lack of confidence—a feeling that you are lucky to be where you are and should not concern yourself with moving forward. Years ago, I can remember an accountant coming to me and saying he wanted a job but did not want to be paid more than $80 a week (as you can see, this was quite a while ago). When I told him he could probably get a job that paid more, he was not interested. "As long as I'm making only $80 a week," he told me. "I know I won't be under that much pressure, and if business gets bad, I won't be laid off."

There is inherent risk in this attitude. The risk is that, as you grow older, your image of yourself might improve and produce a sudden desire to strive for a higher position—by then, it might be too late to make the move you are thinking about. You already will have been pigeonholed and, besides, your record will not demonstrate achievement and advancement.

The point, then, is very simple. If you are going to set career goals, you are better off aiming slightly too high than slightly too low.

THE IMPORTANCE OF WORKING HARD

Nobody would dispute the fact that accounting is hard work, but, as Bob Anderson, my Chicago franchisee, points out, to be highly successful in this field, you really have to go *beyond* the work ethic. "The one thing I've learned about this profession,' says Anderson, "is that if you're not willing to work the longest hours, you're going to hold yourself back." By way of example, Anderson cites an early experience in which he was working in the accounting department of a major corporation but was not terribly pleased with his situation. "There were six accountants on each side of the room," he says, "and they all had 3-piece suits and a calculator. It was a stifling environment and I wanted out."

Anderson eventually got out of this environment, but not without putting in a great deal of extra work. It seems that the assistant treasurer of the company, who was also the manager of two finance companies, had a bookkeeping problem and needed some extra work done. Andersen volunteered. "I did *more* than I had to do," Anderson says, "and the net result was that the assistant treasurer eventually created a full-time position for me as his assistant." From there Anderson became a accounting manager for one of the company's subsidiaries and was subsequently promoted to senior consolidation accountant. Eventually, he assumed the controllership of a smaller company.

Bob Anderson's success path convincingly illustrates what psychologist Charles Garfield refers to as "avoiding the comfort zone." Anderson was a good enough accountant, certainly, to have fit in very nicely in that first niche, but he wanted more. More important, he was willing to do the extra work to move out of that zone. His story is not at all unusual among successful people.

BEING WILLING TO PUT YOURSELF ON THE LINE

"A great many accountants," says Norman Auerbach, "hold themselves back because they are so afraid of being wrong they never make decisions." Auerbach goes so far as to rate the willingness to make decisions as one of the most important factors in a successful accounting career. "You need confidence in your judgment," says

Auerbach. "And you have to be *willing to be wrong*. Nobody—not even the most successful manager—is right *all* the time."

As it happens, Auerbach worked for a firm where "we gave young people the opportunity to make decisions." He adds that decision making does not come naturally to people. "It's something you learn," he says, "if you have basic intelligence."

The problem with making decisions, of course, is that every decision you make entails a certain amount of risk, and because so many decisions in accounting are directly related to the bottom line, the decisions take on all the more importance. Maybe this is why so many accountants shy away from the decision-making aspect of the profession.

What is lacking in many accountants is a quality that publisher Malcolm Forbes chooses to call "imagination." "With some notable exceptions," Forbes told me, "Accountants are too cost conscious and figure conscious to let their imagination go. Too often, they fail to recognize—or even care about—the *significance* of the numbers." Forbes goes on to cite as one of the major failings of accountants in general the failure to give "life" to figures, although he recognizes the problems that accountants are usually up against. "Accounting is such a tough discipline," he says, "that the characteristics required to do the basic work correctly often smother the other ingredients of success."

True enough. The basic operational functions of an accountant can often be so demanding that they could very well, as Forbes says, "smother other ingredients" of success, but, if you are going to rise above the norm, you cannot allow this to happen. At some point, you must look beyond the figures and focus your energy and attention on the lie beneath the figures. "Nothing will you hold you back more in accounting," says Buddy Martin, CPA, partner in the firm of Martin Rosen & Company, "than having tunnel vision. You have to see the whole picture—not just the numbers."

ACCOMPLISHMENT FOR THE "ART" OF IT

It should come as no surprise to you to learn that the overwhelming majority of highly successful people truly love what they do. As Malcolm Forbes, who is probably the best example I know of a businessman who takes enormous pleasure in his work, likes to put it, "If you don't like what you're doing you'll never be successful. I don't think anybody does something really well unless they truly enjoy what they do."

Tom Monaghan, the president and founder of Domino's Pizza, tells an interesting anecdote in his book, *Pizza Tiger*, about a conversation he had with the late Ray Kroc, who once said, "I've never *worked* a day in my life. I've just had fun." Kroc, Monaghan explains, had long been an idol of his and, after nearly 12 years of trying to get an appointment with the McDonald's founder, Monaghan was finally able to set up a meeting. At the time, Kroc was 78 and in failing health, but he and Monaghan exchanged ideas for nearly three hours when Kroc's assistant finally broke in and said that Kroc had another appointment. At this point, Monaghan describes, Kroc leaned forward across his desk and said, "I'm going to give you some advice. You can do anything you want. So what you should do now is slow down and take it easy. Play it safe."

Monaghan could not believe what he was hearing, since it was the exact opposite of what he thought Kroc believed in. "But that wouldn't be any fun," Monaghan finally blurted out, at which point, Kroc grinned, lunged forward, and, pumping Monaghan's hand, exclaimed, "That's just what I hoped you'd say."

What is true for businesspeople as a whole is, of course, true for accountants. But, more than simply loving what they do, successful accountants, as a group, see an element of challenge and romance in virtually everything they do, even the most routine tasks. And why not? Accounting offers the chance to become involved in more aspects of business than other professionals can be involved with: taxes, costs, budgets, and deal making.

"It all depends on how you look at things," says Saul Silverman.

> Take a job as routine as checking bills to verify accuracy. If the only thing you're interested is accuracy, it's drudgery. But if you're looking, with interest, at bills, receipts, freight vouchers, what you're getting is a story. Then, there's more romance. You can follow what's happening.

It is a familiar theme. Some people refer to it as "sinking your teeth into a project." Others liken what *they* do for companies to what surgeons do for sick people. Malcolm Forbes calls it "enjoying the idea of digging meaning out of figures." Issac Assael, CPA and partner of M.R. Weiser & Co., calls it, simply, "the desire for excellence." And Thomas Hurst, who spent much of his accounting career with General Motors before joining our Phoenix office, describes it as simply "an attitude for doing whatever you do well."

Whatever it is, you always manage to feel a certain sense of excitement whenever you are talking about accounting with the top people in the profession.

INTELLECTUAL CURIOSITY

"On my first day of class in college," recalls Harry A. Gilbert, a CPA who headed our Southern Californian operations, "I had a professor who said to us, 'Everybody here will get an A if you take my class and learn to apply your reasoning powers." Gilbert says he's never forgotten that opening day speech and attributes the success he has enjoyed in accounting and business to the fact that he has kept that principle in mind throughouit his business career.

Gilbert remembers, for instance, that soon after he graduated he joined a 40-person CPA firm whose philosophy was a reaffirmation of what his professor had said.

> They preached to us at the firm that when you're through with your work papers on the job and the debits equal the credits, that is only the beginning of the job—that's when you step back and look at it and ask yourself, "Does it make sense? Is it reasonable for the amount of sales that were done in that period?" In other words, what they were looking for was a test of "reasonableness."

What Gilbert is talking about here is possibly the one trait, above all others, that differentiates accountants at the top of the profession from the middle-of-the-road practitioners. "What it all comes down to, I guess," Philip B. Chenok CPA, Past-President of the American Institute of CPAs, told me, "is inquisitiveness." "The most successful accountants I know," says Chenok, "are prone not to accept information without raising questions. And when they raise questions, there is an element of common sense that comes through in their assessment and evaluation." Chenok goes on to say point out that accountants are hardly the only group of professionals for whom inquisitiveness is an important trait. "Almost invariably," he says, "inquisitive people are people who come up with creative ideas."

Let me append to Chenok's statement a brief anecdote about a highly competent accountant I once knew who lost out on a position he wanted very badly—for the very reason we are discussing here, a lack of inquisitiveness, the inability to see beyond the numbers. The accountant had great credentials, but, when the interviewer asked him to talk about his most interesting client—a small southern college—all the accountant could talk about were the numbers. Explained the interviewer to me afterward, "When the candidate didn't know anything, apart from financial data, about a client he'd been working with for several years, I realized I was dealing with somebody who did not have an inquiring mind and didn't have much depth, either."

SUCCESS INGREDIENTS: A SUMMARY

The qualities I have just mentioned are hardly the only ones shared by successful accountants. I have noticed, for instance, that most of the successful accountants I know are positive thinkers. You rarely hear them complaining about their work or about the pressures they are under. Most of them have a healthy sense of humor: they take what they do seriously, but they can laugh at themselves, too. In short, while they may be singleminded about their careers, they are also well-rounded individuals who give the impression that they would be successful in any field.

There is one more quality that I should stress here, if only because it is one that in some ways transcends everything else: your ability to keep your spirit up in the face of frustration, rejection, and outright failure. If there is anything you can say about very successful people as a group, it is that they all know what failure tastes like. Most of the successful people I am friendly with, for instance, have been fired from at least one job, and can point to any number of times in their careers when nothing seemed to be going right for them. It is significant, too, that, according to a survey, a substantial percentage of Americans who had become millionaires by age 35 had also gone bankrupt before they found the financial vehicle that brought them their success.

How are these people different from most people? Briefly, they see failure as an opportunity for learning. As one highly successful salesman I know likes to put it, "I never fail, but sometimes I simply get negative feedback."

TEST YOUR AMBITION QUOTIENT

Do you *really* want to be successful?

I posed this question at the beginning of this chapter and I have tried to help you answer it by pointing out some of the qualities that successful people seem to share.

Below, I have put together a self-test that will further help answer the question. The questions are based on statements from a variety of success articles that I keep on file. I do not claim this test is scientific, but taking it will give you at least some idea of how ambitious you are to be successful.

To take the test, gauge the degree to which each of the statements below applies to you. Answer each question on a scale of 1 to 5, with 1 indicating that the statements does not apply at all to you and 5 indicating the statement very much applies to you.

1.   I truly enjoy working.   _____

2. Given free time, I would rather be out socializing with people than sitting home watching television. _____

3. My first response to a problem is to try to figure out the most practical solution. _____

4. One of the things I like best about work is the challenge of it. _____

5. I believe very strongly in the work ethic. _____

6. I have a strong desire to get things done. _____

7. When there is a difficult situation, I enjoy assuming the responsibility for correcting it. _____

8. I frequently come up with ideas—day and night. _____

9. I'm not satisfied with the success I already enjoy. _____

10. I rarely miss a day of work because of illness. _____

11. I enjoy vacations but after four or five days, I look forward to getting back to work. _____

12. I can usually get along with six hours of sleep. _____

13. I'm interested in meeting people and developing contacts. _____

14. I set high standards for myself in almost everything I do. _____

15. All in all, I consider myself a lucky person. _____

16. I'm not afraid to rely on my instinct when I have to make an important decision. _____

17. I can think of very few situations in my life in which I do not have a great deal of control. _____

18. I recover from setbacks pretty quickly. I don't dwell on them. _____

19. I'm not afraid to admit it when I make a big mistake. _____

20. Achieving success is important to me. _____

HOW TO RATE YOURSELF

Score yourself as follows:

85 to 100—Very high ambition quotient: with the proper skills, you are almost certain to achieve your goals

70 to 84—Higher than average: your chances of achieving your

ambition are very good, provided, that is, you have the talent and skills to go along with your desire

55 to 69—About average: If you have achieved your ambition—or are about to achieve it—it will not be because of your attitude or approach

Below 55—Below average: success, by most people's standards, is not an important goal for you

Getting the Most Out of Yourself

3

Brains, diligence, personality,
and appearance—use any
one of these properly and
you'll get along. Use them all
and you've got power.

A good many years ago, before I started my personnel recruiting company, I attended a daylong seminar at which one of the speakers was a prominent professor who was a tax lawyer and CPA, known in particular for his expertise in a specialized phase of tax law.

I was not at the time—and I am certainly not now—an expert in taxes, but I was interested in tax law, and, even as a very young man, I was a reasonably knowledgeable student on the subject. Yet, I am not embarrassed to admit that from the moment this professor began talking until he finished his presentation 45 minutes later, I was lost—and for a good reason. There was no central thought to his talk, no logical progression of ideas, no theme—just a jumble of section numbers and statements strung together in random fashion. Worse, the professor spoke in a barely audible monotone and looked out at his audience only once or twice during the speech. After he finished his talk, he did not bother to ask if anybody had any questions.

I was disappointed. I had wanted very much to learn about what he had to say, and it troubled me that somebody who knew so much about a subject I wanted to learn more about had absolutely no idea of how to communicate this information—and did not seem to care.

What surprised me more than anything about the speech was how tolerant the audience was. There were about 20 of us in the conference room. I was one of the few accountants—the rest were lawyers and business executives—and it was clear from the way the people were talking after the speech that I was not the only person in the audience who did not understand what the speaker was trying to say. It was also clear that nobody was as upset as I. As the lawyer who had been sitting next to me during the speech put it, "What can you expect? The guy's really an accountant."

As I said, this seminar took place a good many years ago. I mention it here because the comment of the lawyer has always troubled me—mainly because I have heard it in one form or another over and over again in all the years I have been involved in the accounting profession. Unfortunately, it is a comment that reflects the image many people have of accountants.

The image I am talking about depicts accountants as introverts who are more comfortable with numbers than they are with people, and whose contributions to the companies they serve are confined primarily to making sure the numbers add up properly on the balance sheet. Here is how writer Mark Stevens describes this image in *The Big Eight:*

> You can spot the technicians a mile away. Just walk through the halls of The Big Eight and peek inside the offices. You'll see all kinds of men and women. Technicians are the ones who look as though they've been locked in a library since puberty. It's a strange breed: introverted, glazy-eyed little men, they dress in sober fashion even by Big Eight standards, stare at their shoes, and carry themselves with icy formality.

Granted, Mr. Stevens is generalizing here, and I surely do not mean to suggest that his description applies to the accounting profession as a whole. I know hundreds of accountants quite well, and, outside of the fact that, as a group, they tend to be a little more conservative and precise than the world at large, I find it impossible to make generalizations about them. In their appearance, their personality, and their outlook on life, you will find as much diversity as among other groups of professionals. Some are quiet and reserved. Others are boisterous and aggressive. Some have sedentary hobbies, like stamp collecting. Others go in for more adventurous pursuits, like skiing or mountain climbing. I know of a California accountant who races motorcycles on the weekends, although I don't think he advertises this fact to his clients.

These considerations apart, the fact remains that accountants do suffer from an image problem—particularly, I think, in management accounting. A study conceived by my company and conducted by Burke Marketing found that some corporate executives perceived management accountants as "glorified bookkeepers."

Mind you, we are not dealing here with reality, but with the way people perceive other people. The facts are clear. The business community perceives accountants differently from the way accountants perceive themselves. I base this view on more than my personal experience. (On more occasions than I could ever count, I have had employers looking for an accountant say to me, "I don't want a 'typical' accountant. I want somebody with personality.") I base it also on the results of the Burke Marketing Research survey conducted expressly for this book. One striking feature of that survey was the difference between the way accountants perceive themselves and the way other business people perceive accountants.

For example, when we asked respondents to specify the degree to which they agreed with the statement, "Public accountants have the ability to get along well with people," some 41 per cent of CPA partners answered "very strongly." When the same question was put to top corporate management, only 10 per cent agreed "very strongly"—a difference of some 30 percentage points. And, when personnel directors were asked how strongly they agreed with the statement, only 14 per cent answered "very strongly."

The poll turned up a similar divergence of views on the subject of communication skills. About 45 per cent of the CPA partners we queried agreed "strongly" with the statement that "Public accountants have good communications skills," but only 14 per cent of corporate personnel directors shared this feeling, and only 6 per cent of top corporate management felt that accountants have good communication skills.

In the case of management accountants, the divergence we found was not as striking. In general, however, the financial people we spoke to—the chief financial officers and the CPA partners—had a higher opinion of management accountants than the nonfinancial people.

What do these figures tell us? In short, they tell us that in certain key areas—communications and interpersonal relations, to cite just two—there is a fundamental and crucial gap between the way accountants, particularly public accountants, perceive themselves and the way they are perceived by top management. They also tell us that if you are interested in getting ahead in accounting, a good place to start is with the image you project to the rest of the world.

IMAGE: IT STARTS WITH YOUR APPEARANCE

Years ago, I had a morning meeting with a financial executive of a large industrial company, at the end of which I observed something I have never forgotten. The executive excused himself from his office and came back moments later with a change of clothing. Throughout the morning, he had been wearing a light-colored plain suit. Now, he was wearing a dark pinstripe. Why did he change clothes? His luncheon date that afternoon was with a Boston banker!

For better or worse, all of us are judged—to some degree at least—by our appearance. And, whether we want to admit it or not, most of us base our own judgments on appearance too. True, once we get to know somebody well, our impressions become based on more meaningful criteria, but the problem in business is that many of the people we deal with we see only now and then. This is particularly the case, I think, with accountants. If you are working for a CPA firm, for instance, you probably see many clients three or four times a year, so you need to ask yourself whether you are making a strong enough and favorable enough impression. As Patricia Frechtman, a personnel management consultant, says, "You never get a second chance to make a good first impression."

Research more than bears out the relationship between your appearance and how people perceive you. Studies by psychologist Ellen Berscheid, an expert in the psychology of attractiveness, for instance, show that if people consider you attractive, they are also likely to consider you kind, genuine, sincere, and interesting. Another set of studies has shown that if you are a male executive who stands over 6 feet 2 inches tall, you probably earn a 12 per cent higher salary than a man under 6 feet. In one of the most interesting studies done on the subject, it was found that panhandlers who are reasonably well dressed will bring in more than shabbily dressed panhandlers.

Granted, not everybody can look like a movie star, and your height is something you really cannot do anything about. But, there are many aspects of your appearance over which you have a great deal of control. I am talking, in particular, about the way you dress, the way you carry yourself, the way you speak: in short, the image you generate whenever you are with other people. Observes Frank M. Davidson, a Harvard MBA and CPA who formerly headed our Northwestern offices, "As basic as it may seem, the general image you project is one of the things that a great many accountants simply overlook."

The relationship between the image you project and career success in business is such that more than 100 companies nationwide specialize in telling businessmen and businesswomen how to get the most out of their appearance. So, perhaps not to you, but certainly to the people you have to deal with in your job, appearance *does* count. For this reason alone, you should do everything in your power to look as good as you possibly can.

Most accountants, in my experience, fail to give enough thought to their business wardrobes. I'm not sure *why* this should be, but I suspect it has something to do with a feeling that accountants (unlike, say, salespeople) are not *expected* to dress well. I could not disagree more. As consultant Susan Bixler points out, when you dress poorly, your credibility suffers. As James Peters, national director of recruiting for Ernst & Whinney, says, "On the job, new accountants are expected to dress like the rate we're charging for them, so clients feel that they're getting a professional person." Consider, too, the results of a survey done by the New York University Graduate School in which nearly 100 per cent of the personnel consultants and executive recruiters queried agreed that dressing well is important to career success.

Exactly *how* you dress, of course, will depend largely on the sort of firm you work for and the region of the country in which you live, but in most cases you will be expected to dress in a conservative and businesslike style. Most firms like to see their men in dark, traditionally styled suits and their women in tailored suits and dresses.

The reasons are obvious. "It isn't just for *our* sake that we are very concerned about the appearance of our accountants," says Robert Maynard, CPA, a partner and national director of human resources for Price Waterhouse. "We have to think about the reactions our clients are going to have to somebody who wears a rumpled suit and looks scraggly. Appearance is one of the things we look at very carefully when we hire candidates."

Regardless of the guidelines that prevail in your particular company or firm, the basic rule for you to keep in mind is this: everything in your wardrobe should in one way or another *enhance* your image. Everything you wear, in other words, should make you appear substantial, educated, trustworthy, confident—all the qualities you need for success.

I suggest, to begin with, that you go through your wardrobe at your first opportunity. As you do, look through every piece of clothing you wear when you are at work. At the same time, ask yourself whether that piece of clothing, whether it is a shirt, a blouse, a suit, a tie, or a pair of shoes, is doing anything to enhance your image as a professional. Then, think to yourself how you *feel* when you wear this item. When wearing this item, in other words, do you feel comfortable and important? I know a highly successful accountant who spends nearly

$600 for his suits. When somebody suggested that he might look just as good if he wore a $300 suit, he replied, "Yes, but I wouldn't *feel* as good."

In the event you yourself do not have a sense of what clothes suit you best, I suggest one of two things: (1) find a clothing store with an excellent reputation for conservative professional clothes and put yourself in their hands; (2) buy one of the several books out on the market today that deal with business dress. None of these books are written specifically for accountants, but they do give advice that applies to professional people in general. One of the things these books will preach to you is that it is better to have a few high quality clothing items than a closet full of bargain basement specials. Tailoring, in particular, is crucial. That is why, if you have an unusual build, you are almost always better off having your clothes made to order than you are buying them readymade.

This brings up one of the cardinal rules of dressing: designing your wardrobe around your build and coloring. If you are on the heavy side, stick with darker colors—they will give you a thinner appearance. If you are on the short and stocky side, choose pin stripes and, at all costs, stay away from plaid sports jackets and slacks. Plaids, remember, will widen your appearance. If you have a pale complexion, do not dress in anything too dark: it will merely accentuate your paleness. When it comes to colors, stick to basics: mainly grays, blues, and browns. "Since accountants deal with something near and dear to their clients' hearts—money—," says Sharon Bixler, "they must dress to show they have both feet on the ground."

As far as styles go, single-breasted suits are fine for average-sized men, but I have noticed a lot of the taller men in accounting favoring dark double-breasted suits. In either case, make sure the fit does justice to the style. Important checkpoints for men are the shoulders and the waist. The shoulder seam of the jacket should rest on the point of the shoulder, and the trousers should be comfortable without being too baggy. A good suggestion: have the tailor pin the trousers to the fit that *looks* good, and then sit down to make sure the fit will be comfortable as well.

When it comes to accessories, quality is just as important as it is for suits and jackets. In the case of shirts, so is fit. Some men find that standard-size shirts do not always fit their necks well and so they have their shirts custommade. I think this is a good investment, especially when you consider that your collar is something that people will notice every time they look you in the eye. Keep shirt colors simple—white is best, but light blue or cream are okay, for a change—and never wear short-sleeved dress shirts, no matter how hot it gets.

Select your ties with care and always with an eye for coordinating your choice with other parts of your wardrobe. One of the best dressed men I know always makes it a point, when he is buying a new suit or sport jacket, to buy a couple of good ties that blend well with that particular suit. If you are not sure of your ability to choose such a tie, let somebody whose taste you *do* trust make the choices. Above all, avoid knit, polyester, or very loud ties.

When you are buying a belt, keep the buckle simple and, again, spend a little more for quality. When you are buying socks, it is a good idea to buy several pairs (always calf-length, of course) of the same color. This is will prevent the possibility of showing up for work one day with a pair of mismatched socks.

For women, the guidelines are no less specific. Patricia Frechtman suggests tailored suits, nicely cut, in a soft blue, gray, or brown material. "These styles," she says, "always look businesslike." She also advises a blouse with a button-down collar and a silk scarf or one with its own bow that ties softly at the neck. Footwear, she adds, "should be simple."

The most important thing for women in accounting, advises Patricia Frechtman, is to dress in good taste. "Where jewelry is concerned," she says, "you're better off with too little than too much. Stick to plain gold jewelry or pearls and avoid clinking bracelets or flashy dinner rings." And, while she insists that women do *not* have to hide their femininity, she does warn against wearing anything that might be considered provocative, such as see-through blouses, low necklines, or tight-fitting skirts with slits. "Remember," she says, "If you want to be treated as a professional, you have to *look* like a professional."

One final observation about your wardrobe has to do with its flexibility. If you have to travel to different parts of the country, make sure you have the appropriate clothing for any major changes in climate you are likely to encounter when you get off the plane. As cold as it might be in the Northeast, the last thing you want to be wearing when you arrive in Southern California is a thick wool suit. It is also a good idea to slightly vary the *style* of your clothing according to the region you're visiting. Business executives in the West and Southwest tend to dress more casually than their Eastern counterparts. And, while I would not recommend to an Easterner that he or she arrive at a meeting in Dallas or Houston in a cowboy shirt and string tie, it is worthwhile—if you are going to be going back to the same place time after time—to dress in a manner that will not emphasize the fact that you are from a different region of the country.

BEYOND YOUR WARDROBE

Your appearance, of course, involves more than what you wear. You can spend a small fortune on your wardrobe, but your appearance will still suffer if you neglect your grooming, your complexion, and your general physical shape, and, if you are a woman, if you are not careful with your makeup. Let us look at a few guidelines.

YOUR FACE

The main thing to be said about your facial appearance is that you should be comfortable with the way you look. To be sure, you do not have to look like a movie star to move ahead in accounting, but, at the same time, you do not want your face to interfere with your career progress.

As you undoubtedly know, more and more executives these days—male and female alike—are going in for cosmetic surgery—facelifts and surgery around the eyes, in particular. Their rationale is that looking better—and younger—gives them more confidence and enables them to function more effectively at their jobs. My own feeling about cosmetic surgery—and it is a feeling shared by many people who counsel executives on how to look better—is that you should seek it only when there is something about your physical appearance that is a major source of embarrassment or discomfort to you.

What I *do* advocate, though, is that you pay close attention to your teeth, for if there is anything you want to feel confident about, it is your smile. A rising executive at one of the major CPA firms was unhappy and stymied by the gaps between his teeth. He spent a great deal of money to have his front teeth capped and insists to this day that his rise in the firm since the dental work was done has more than paid for the investment.

Let me also add a word about shaving. Nearly everybody (unless he has a beard) shaves in the morning, and some men have beards that are light enough so that, if they have an engagement at night, they still look clean-shaven. If, though, you are one of those men with a thick five o'clock shadow, it is important that you keep some shaving gear at your office and that you shave again whenever you have important engagements at night. It is not only that not being clean-shaven detracts from your appearance. It is more that, when you need a shave, you *look* tired, and, as you well know, you do not feel as fresh, either.

More and more male executives have begun using blush, a kind of makeup that gives added color to the face. In some cases, I suppose—if you have unusual pallor to your skin—it may not be a bad idea, but whatever you do, go easy, and make sure the makeup does not show. It is better, if you have an unusually pale complexion, to spend a little more time *outdoors.*

For women, makeup is particularly critical, and while less is better than more, not enough, as Patricia Frechtman advises, could pose a problem, too. She suggests a happy medium. "When used properly," she says, "cosmetics enhance a woman's best features and hide her worst features." If you are not confident about makeup, she goes on to advise, you should seek the help of a professional. "In any department store across the country," she says, "there are trained personnel who can help you make the most of your makeup."

YOUR HAIR

Numerous studies have shown that your hair affects the image people have of you as much as anything else about your appearance. Many people, for instance, automatically associate a slick-backed look with criminal activity. Others look at wild and unruly hair and immediately think of instability. Still others will look at a man with a severe crewcut and assume that he must have been a Marine. Are these judgments accurate? Of course not. But they exist, and you have to live with them.

Whatever hairstyle you choose, make sure it is one that works best for your features and your type of hair. Do not be hesitant about spending a few extra dollars for a barber or a stylist who can give you the best look. Needless to say, your hair should always be clean and free of dandruff.

I should mention something about hairpieces for men, if only to press my position that you are almost always better off avoiding them. In the first place, all but the most expensive hairpieces—the ones that can cost several thousand dollars—almost invariably appear artificial. Second, hairpieces can be distracting, and some people tend to stop concentrating on the man they are talking to and pay more attention to the hairpiece.

As far as women go, I yield again to Patricia Frechtman, who stresses the importance of a natural hairstyle that requires little upkeep. "Your hair shouldn't hang down in your eyes or cover your face," she says. "And if you're wearing hair combs, they should be simple, and their color should blend with your hair. If your color is *not* your natural color, make sure you have a regular appointment for coloring."

She gives a final piece of advice to women on the subject of hair.

"Don't play with your hair," she says. "Many women do this when they're nervous, and it's a distracting habit. The best way to avoid the habit is to have well-groomed hair that stays in place and does nothing that might detract from your image."

Moustaches and beards are touchy subjects in many firms. I know of accountants who have grown beards in order to appear wiser, but I know just as many accounting partners who see beards as a sign of nonconformity and do not encourage beards among junior staff members. Moustaches, on the other hand, have a somewhat higher rate of acceptance in the older, larger firms. Still, if I were a young accountant looking to generate a winning image in today's market, I would wear neither a moustache nor a beard, unless I wanted to conceal a scar or other facial defect. My philosophy in business has always been to play the odds: When something cannot do me any good, there is always the chance that it will do me harm. Why gamble?

DON'T FORGET YOUR NAILS

There is not too much to be said about the appearance and condition of your nails, but the little bit that needs to be said is nonetheless important, particularly for men. Unlike women, for whom nail care is one of the basics of good grooming, many men are unaware of the degree to which poorly cared for nails can take away from one's appearance.

Basic nail care for men consists of making sure your mails are always clean and well shaped and that your cuticles are pushed back and trimmed. An inexpensive nailbrush is all you need to keep your nails clean, but you should spend a little extra to buy a basic nail kit—nail clipper, cuticle scissors, nail file—for weekly self-maintenance. I would also recommend that you get a manicure (although without polish), not only for the appearance of your nails but for the basic conditioning that a good manicure provides. Women should not wear their nails too long, should not use too bright a polish, and should *never* get caught with chipped polish. A small bottle of polish remover is probably a better safeguard than polish used to patch up a chip.

YOUR PHYSICAL SHAPE

Nobody expects you to be built like Clint Eastwood or Jane Fonda, but most of the highly successful accountants I know radiate a sense of fitness and energy, and any number of studies indicate that the kind of physical shape you are in has a direct bearing on your career progress.

We have found over and over again in our own studies, for instance, that all things being equal, an obese person is much less likely to be hired than a nonobese person. I am not saying there are no accounting partners who could not stand to take off 20 pounds, but I am willing to bet that if you surveyed the leading partners in the top 20 accounting firms throughout the country, you would find that relatively few of them are substantially overweight and that most of them do something —whether jogging, swimming, or walking—to keep trim. Says Charles J. Wolff, CPA, who is associated with our Phoenix office, "If you neglect your health and appearance in accounting, you're sabotaging your career. And one of the best things any accountant who isn't already exercising can do is to get into some regular fitness activity."

Apart from what it does to enhance your appearance and your health, a regular fitness activity, whether it is swimming, tennis, squash, or running, gives you a built-in means of expanding your contacts and of dealing with the pressures inherent in accounting. "The one thing I regret," says Saul Silverman, "is that I stopped taking part in sports as soon as I got busy in my career. I see now that if I had played, say, tennis or golf I could have benefited in many ways. I would have had an activity I enjoyed, and I would have met more people. One of the best things an accountant, man or woman, can do today is to become involved in some sport."

YOUR IMAGE: OTHER CONSIDERATIONS

Your appearance encompasses factors that go beyond the way you look and dress. Recently, for instance, I saw a job application from an accountant who had been working for one of the best-known CPA firms but had been fired. The reason, according to the application: "I drove a pickup."

Firing an accountant because he drives a pickup truck may seem harsh. Then again, think about it. If you headed a $100 million company, would you be comfortable with an accountant who came to see you in a pickup truck? I doubt it. So do not overlook the little things. The car you drive, the kind of stationery you use, the design of your business card, the message you put on your telephone answering machine—all of it contributes to your image, and none of it should be taken for granted.

In this regard, I would suggest that if you—or your company—can afford it, you should travel first class. This may sound extravagant to you, but there are some sound reasons for flying first class, apart from the added comfort of the flight. First of all, traveling first class massages your ego: When you *think* you're important, you *become* important. Second, the added room you have in first class makes it easier for you to catch up on your paperwork when you are traveling.

Probably the key advantage of traveling first class over coach is that you stand a good chance of meeting business people who could become clients or valuable contacts in the future. While flying first class, I have met any number of people who were in a position to give our company business. One of them, the executive vice president of a leading Pittsburgh corporation, has given our franchise there a great deal of business over a long period of time.

The last time I flew to Europe, I flew the Concorde. While waiting for the plane in the Concorde lounge at Heathrow, I met an executive from one of the leading industrial firms in England, whose firm just happened to need financial people for its headquarters in London and its affiliate in Hong Kong. I am sure our British people will be hearing from that firm.

Mind you, I never actively solicit business—and neither should you. If I meet someone who does not ask me what I do, I am content to talk about the weather or the news of the day. But when you are sitting next to someone on a flight that is longer than a few hours, chances are the conversation is eventually going to come around to business.

The same principle holds true for hotels and restaurants. If you are visiting an out-of-town client, you want the hotel you stay at to reflect an image of success. Again, there is a cost factor to consider, but the difference between the truly first-rate hotels and the typical business person's hotel usually is not that great and seems to me to be well worth the difference. Most of the most successful executives I know have become regular customers at a handful of very good restaurants and will go to those restaurants when they are entertaining. When you are out of town, it is not as easy to become known at the better restaurants, but you might consider dropping by the restaurant in person to make your reservation, to choose the table you want, and to give the ma&C0tre d'hôtel your card—along with a tip. One more thing to think about when you are taking clients out to dinner and driving a car is to tip the parking attendant a little extra in advance in order to get a spot that will enable you to get your car immediately.

DEVELOPING YOUR INTERPERSONAL SKILLS

As it happens, our Burke survey findings do not paint all that bleak a picture of an accountant's interpersonal skills. Except for the fact that 30 per cent of top management had negative things to say about the interpersonal skills of their internal accountants, the general feeling as it emerged from our Burke survey was that accountants are neither here nor there when it comes to the ability to get along well with people, which makes an accountant who can combine interpersonal skills with technical competence an accountant with a rosy future.

"We've had many absolutely brilliant people working for us, and we still do," says Richard Hickok.

> The brilliant ones who have not met with success simply did not know how to get along well with clients. As an example, we once sent an accountant to work with the payroll manager of a client, and the accountant was so arrogant he made the payroll manager appear stupid. We quickly got a call from the client telling us to take the accountant off that job. That kind of a track record is not going to get an accountant very far in this profession.

Denis J. O'Leary, CPA, director of personnel of KMG Main Hurdman, (now Peat Marwick Main & Co.) feels much the same way as Hickok.

> Technical skills are most important during the first five or six years of your career, but after that time, progress depends largely on how well you relate to people: how you relate to the people above you, how well you supervise, how well you're able to deal with the client and the client's personnel—in short, your ability to communicate with all people. That's where we draw the distinction between the accountants who are going to move forward versus the ones who are not going any further. Technical requirements are always going to be necessary, but as you move up, the interpersonal skills take on more and more importance.

To be sure, there is nothing complicated about interpersonal skills. *Skills,* in fact, is a misleading word, since it implies that getting along well with people is something you learn, like a course in advanced math. Basically, it is a matter of being courteous, pleasant, and understanding in your dealings with other people. It is *caring* genuinely about other people—being sensitive to their feelings. It means being tactful when you are pointing out a mistake to a secretary, and being patient and understanding if, say, a company auditor has not put together the figures you are looking for.

It is also recognizing that, regardless of the situation, your best interests are rarely served if you have to resort to tactics that irritate people. "More often than most accountants realize," says Graham Thompson, CA, in charge of our Calgary franchise, "accountants with personalities that grate on others are their own worst enemies. They don't realize that when their personality grates on others, they get frozen out of information and gradually they begin to lose authority."

I have my own theory about why some accountants have a difficult time getting along with people, and it has to do with the kind of training accountants receive. As an accountant, you are trained to be inquisitive, almost to the point of being suspicious. You are trained to look for oversights, deceptions—even frauds. Some accountants, however, let this suspiciousness carry over into other areas of their work. Their suspicions prevent them from communicating well and from delegating. (Some accountants are suspicious of subordinates they themselves have hired.) I might add, too, that unless accountants can keep this tendency to be suspicious from taking over their personalities, their overall performance suffers.

There are two interpersonal skills I would like to mention here, primarily because they are qualities that many people overlook. The first is being a good listener. The second is having a sense of humor. As you probably know, most people are not very good at listening, and the reason, psychologists tell us, is that listening is not as easy as most people think. The average person, for instance, speaks at a rate of about 125 words per minute, but most of us think at the rate of 400 to 500 words per minute, and we can listen at the speed of 600 words per minute. As a result, the natural tendency of the listener is to let the mind stray. Another problem with listening is that many people, instead of listening to what is being said to them, tend to think about what they are going to say next. This would explain an observation of mine that ears are so sensitive they sometimes hear things that are never said.

Psychologists insist that the only way to improve listening skills is to concentrate on them. You have to resist the natural tendency of your mind to drift, and you must resist the temptation to concentrate on your reply. You have to think about it, concentrate on it, and, most of all, care about it.

As far as a sense of humor goes, it should suffice to say that, even as an accountant, you are entitled to have one, and that in many situations having a sense of humor can make the difference in your ability to get through difficult situations. "A sense of humor is particularly important for women," says Caryn Newman, a CPA who is now a financial executive for a department store chain.

> I can remember any number of occasions in which a receptionist had trouble accepting the fact that I was really an accountant. When I was a public accountant, I once went to a television station

client and was asked by the receptionist if I was the "talent" for the talk show. Sure, it's easy to get disturbed in that kind of a situation, but what would it gain me?

All told, then, developing interpersonal skills requires little skill in and of itself, but does require a great deal of practice. It is mostly a matter of making the effort to get along with the people you deal with. Here are a few guidelines, some of them perhaps obvious, but all of them important:

1. Smile at people when you first meet them
2. Look them in the eye (but do not overdo it)
3. Do not work too hard to make a good impression
4. Do not talk too much about yourself—show an interest in others
5. Make it a point to listen to what people are saying to you (rather than thinking up your reply)
6. Show courtesy to everyone
7. Have a sense of humor

I will have more to say about speaking and writing as important tools for marketing yourself in Chapter Seven. For now, it is enough to recognize that of all the skills you develop, few will do more to enhance your career progress than the ability to communicate effectively.

BECOME AN AUTHORITY

No matter what else your personality projects about you, people should perceive you as an authority, particularly when it comes to matters of accounting and finance. Regardless of what your job may be, you should be able to discuss such topics as economics and inflation intelligently. You should know something about business conditions in general. People expect that much from an accountant, and if you do not demonstrate this knowledge, you will not inspire confidence.

The best way to become an authority, of course, is to read. If you're not doing so already, you should subscribe to many of the major business publications, such as *The Wall Street Journal, Forbes, Business Week,* and *Fortune* and to the major accounting journals, such as the *Journal of Accounting, Management Accounting,* and *The Practical Accountant.* I would also subscribe to the newsletters relating to your specific specialty. Set aside at least an hour each day in order to read (but do not do it at work). You want to be able to discuss matters with your colleagues and your superiors. You should be able to read quickly. If you are a slow reader, take a speed-reading course. You might also want to consider using a highlight pen to call attention to important thoughts and ideas.

In my career, I have found it extremely useful to keep a permanent clipping file of articles, reports, and any general information related to my business. I started this "morgue"—the newspaper term for a permanent file—more than 30 years ago, and it has grown to fill more than half a dozen large filing cabinets. I collect anything I can get my hands on that has to do with hiring or managing people. I even collect appropriate humor.

Some of my friends tell me I overdo these things, and maybe I do. On the other hand, whenever I have had to prepare a speech or give testimony before a congressional committee, write an article, or appear on radio or TV, I have never been at a loss for relevant data. I get a kick, too, out of having reporters and authors ask me to check my file for material on subjects they are writing about. The fact that I am happy to oblige makes them that much more cooperative when it comes to supporting my company's public relations.

Apart from becoming an authority on the subjects that relate to accounting, I recommend strongly that you develop and cultivate an interest in a field or area that has nothing to do with accounting— something you enjoy that could also enhance your career prospects.

Consider the late Dan G. Kramer, CPA, who had been the managing editor of the *CPA Journal* for 10 years. For 23 years before becoming an editor, he was a partner at Oppenheim, Appel, Dixon & Co. Karmer always loved classical music and at Oppenheim found himself developing a broad variety of music clients. As Kramer explained to me:

> I'm not saying that my interest in music created this business for our firm, but it did enable me to capitalize on it once the opportunity presented itself. I was able to talk with music people. They were comfortable with me. That's why I've always urged accountants to develop a broad variety of interests. It can't help but have some influence on an accounting career.

On the subject of becoming an authority, I would urge you, in the event you have neglected it, to become proficient at two of the most basic skills an accountant can have: The first is bookkeeping; the second is basic math. The reason being proficient at bookkeeping is so important, even in this age of the computer, is that, somehow, somewhere, you are going to be involved, as an accountant, with a bookkeeper, and the last thing you want to do is embarrass yourself by calling attention to a "mistake" when there is none. It happened to me once, early in my career, and I have never forgotten it.

Then there is proficiency in math. It constantly surprises me that many accountants are not particularly good mathematicians. I know that I myself am not a crackerjack mathematician, but I have worked hard at it, and I have become a little better than adequate. Today, with calculators a basic tool in the industry, it is getting harder and harder to find young accountants who can do simple addition, subtraction, division, and multiplication without the calculator.

An accountant creates a better impression by doing basic calculations rapidly and without a machine. It is simply a fact that, if you are in a restaurant or are buying something in a store, the people with you will be favorably impressed when they see how quickly and accurately you can audit the bill. The reality is that you do not need to be a great mathematician to be an accountant, but the public does not always perceive things that way.

GET TO KNOW THE COMPUTER

You don't have to be a computer expert to know that most business functions today are being computerized, especially in accounting. A number of firms are sending auditors equipped with portable computers to their clients. A recent AICPA survey indicates that the number of CPA firms using computers has increased tenfold since 1981, as compared with only a twofold increase from 1974 to 1981. Citing again from our Burke survey, we found that virtually everyone we queried—nearly 95 per cent—recognized the importance of having some knowledge of the computer. Interestingly, CPA partners and CFOs found knowing the computer more important for management accountants than for public accountants.

The computer has freed accounting firms from much of the computational drudgery that used to be such a part of the day-to-day routine in accounting. This has enabled the profession to become a good deal more sophisticated and accountants to broaden the scope of their services to clients—to do more analyzing and consulting. Much financial planning today is done with computers, and in public accounting, the computer is so important that some firms now have computers to audit the computers.

When I talk about learning the computer, I am talking about two things: one, learning the basic principles of computer sciences, such as language; and, two, learning how to operate microcomputers and minicomputers. The idea in each case should be to gain knowledge about computers and what they do so that you can take an active role in your firm's computer operations.

Another skill you might have to learn as part of your computer education, in the event that you have not already learned it, is typing. Curiously enough, it is their inability to type that is keeping many executives from using computer terminals, but accountants cannot afford this kind of resistance. If it is of any consolation to you, typing, if you apply yourself, is not difficult to learn.

In any case, becoming comfortable with the computer will take a commitment. Alex Cohen, a CPA and attorney who is the publisher of *The Practical Accountant,* estimates that it takes about a year to learn the basics of computer science. He recommends not only buying a home computer but reading the computer journals, attending trade shows, and taking computer courses. I think it is a good idea for accountants to make the computer a hobby. Working with a home computer can be as much fun as chess, bridge, coin collecting, or music, and it will have a direct bearing on your performance at work. You could set up home programs to monitor your investments or you could try to set up programs that relate specifically to your firm's operations.

Equally important, if possible, is to get involved whenever there is going to be a computer installation or revision in your firm. Michael Goldstein did this in the early 1970s when a firm he was with decided to put in a computer, and Goldstein insists that his knowledge of computers was one of the principal factors in his rise to managing partner with Laventhol & Horwath.

The point is, as computers become more and more a fixture in American businesses, management is going to have to rely more and more on accountants to become resident experts. Do not get left out.

BUILD A CONTACT CLUB

It's axiomatic that nobody gets to the top, or even near the top, without help from other people. Indeed, I can think of several successful people, not only in accounting but in other fields, whose chief ability, really, is the ability to capitalize on the people they know. They are not "using people" in the way one normally interprets the phrase. They not only rely on others for help and favors, but they give a great deal of help and do favors themselves. That is an important reason why they are successful. "In the end, it comes down to having an interest in people," says Dan Kramer. "A partner of Oppenheim used to say that if you multiplied the number of friends you had before you were 40 by a certain factor, you could probably estimate how successful you're going to be. The idea was that friends, aside from their important life values, are likely to be the best sources of business."

I consider building contacts so basic to career success that you should be systematic about it. Whenever you meet somebody new, you should write that person's name and business on a 3″ × 5″ file card or, better still, use your personal computer. If you both feel that you are in a position to help each other, try to meet socially. If you are in a position to help the person, try to do it early in the relationship. It will then be much easier for you to go to that person if you need a favor in the future. It is particularly important for you to build contacts in the company for which you work. It is not necessary to force yourself on anyone, but do not be timid about introducing yourself to top management in the appropriate situation.

This process is called *networking,* and one accountant who has a lot to say on the subject is William Aiken, who stresses the importance of *giving* as well as taking from the network. "What I tell the young professionals," says Aiken, "is that a network is like investing in securities. If you keep taking from the principal investment, eventually there will nothing there to generate interest." So you cannot just take. You have to keep investing in the network, helping people.

Aiken stresses, too, the importance not only of cultivating contacts but of making sure that you do not abuse the relationship by making it too one-sided. "In networking," he says, "the worst thing you can do is to get into a pattern in which the only time you're calling on people is when you need a favor from them. You have to keep in contact with people even when things are going well."

REMEMBER, YOU'RE A PROFESSIONAL

Accounting, by its very nature, calls for confidentiality and integrity. Should the people you work with, or for, begin to doubt your ability to keep sensitive information confidential, you will find your horizons extremely limited. Whatever else you do in your job, you must earn and maintain the image of professionalism, honesty, and trustworthiness. An accountant without these qualities is like an athlete without reflexes.

You demonstrate these qualities in any number of ways. For instance, you should make it a cardinal rule never to gossip about either your clients or your firm, regardless of how interesting the information you have might be to other people and of how "harmless" you might think the information is. I cannot tell you how often I have seen accountants get themselves into trouble with loose conversation about a company they happen to be working for or a client they are auditing. In all firms, there is a written or unwritten rule that you do not talk about company business outside the shop. Yes, you can discuss economics or taxes or any number of general topics, but, when it comes to inside information, the rule is very simple. You simply do not talk about it.

There is an even more practical reason for being careful about confidentiality. As an accountant, you come across a great deal of confidential information. If you can demonstrate early in your career that you can be trusted with that information, you will be entrusted with more; and the more confidential information you have in your mental bank, the stronger your position will be to come up with suggestions and recommendations.

Beyond confidentiality, there is the question of ethics—a question that is more important today in accounting than ever before, given the problems the accounting profession went through during the 1960s and early 1970s. Because lawsuits against firms are on the increase, companies of all sizes are policing themselves far more vigorously than ever before, and good firms have little patience with employees whose ethics are dubious.

Ethical problems can arise in a number of ways. Usually, though, when accountants find themselves in an ethical dilemma, it is because of a situation they did not create. One accountant I interviewed recalled a controllership position he once held in a company whose president made it a practice of reporting accounts receivable to the bank on sales that had not yet been booked. "The company had cash flow problems," explained the controller, "and this was the president's way of getting additional loans from the bank. The trouble in this situation was that my signature was on the line."

The controller in this instance did what any ethical—and intelligent —accountant would have done in the same situation. He recognized that putting his signature on a false report not only was unethical but also could have a serious impact on his career. So, he told the president he was not going to take part in this financial charade. Predictably, the controller was forced to quit his job, and, predictably, the company eventually went out of business. The controller, by the way, has become quite successful.

I recall another situation that a chief financial officer from a public company in the Midwest told me about. The CFO had been there only a short time when the chairman of the board called him in and told him how a 10Q was to be prepared for the SEC. The company was contemplating a merger, and the chairman wanted the records to look better. The CFO refused and was fired, but here again, by protecting his own integrity, this executive made the right career move. The merger did take place, but none of the executives in the company were retained after the merger. What is more, there were a number of investigations following the merger. In the meantime, we managed to get the CFO a better job—a job he still has—with a far better company.

The message here is clear. As an accountant, you cannot afford even the slightest of indiscretions, for it takes very little in the way of loss of trust to shatter a career. I have known of CPAs who have lost their licenses, not because they were dishonest, but because they used poor judgment, and sometimes the motivation was merely to help a friend. Do not make the same mistake.

Getting on the Right Career Path

4

Planning doesn't necessarily
make things happen, but it
certainly encourages things
to happen.

Career planning is one of those concepts that looks wonderful on paper. First, you establish an objective—what you want to achieve in your professional career. Then, you set up a plan that outlines the steps designed to lead you to this objective. You build in some means of measuring your progress. Finally, you set up some sort of contingency plan.

No doubt there are successful accountants today whose careers typify the kind of planning I have described—accountants who knew early what they wanted to do and then went on to achieve their objectives according to the timetable they had established. However, most of the successful accountants I know of have had careers that, in retrospect, do not fall into such a tidy pattern.

I know successful accountants who started in public accounting, moved into management accounting, moved back into public accounting, and ended up going out on their own. I know successful accountants who started in public accounting convinced they would be there for only a few years and wound up twenty years later as managing partner in the firm. I know successful management accountants who are still with the firm they entered twenty years ago. I know successful management accountants who have changed firms every three or four years over the past twenty years. I know of a partner in a major firm who left accounting in order to sell insurance for four years, only to return to public accounting. Finally, I know any number of accountants who became successful by getting *out* of accounting.

Does this mean that I consider a career plan a waste of time? Hardly! Having some sort of career plan, obviously, is as important in accounting as it is in any profession. In fact, a survey among high-ranking financial officers at Minnesota-based corporations, conducted by Charles L. Squires, vice-president of Robert Half of Minnesota, showed that more than 80 per cent of the corporate officers polled considered it important for a financial executive to have a career plan. Interestingly enough, only 52 per cent of the officers queried said that they themselves had followed career plans. "What this obviously means," observes Squires, "is that experience has apparently convinced the officers who have a career plan the value of it."

What do I mean by career plan? Nothing complicated, to be sure. Having a career plan means having a reasonably specific idea of where you eventually want your career to take you and how you intend to get there. Having such a plan, I should quickly point out, does not necessarily mean being locked into that plan and never deviating from it. But, without such a plan, you are in the same boat as someone trying to build a house without blueprints.

What is more, career planning is not something you do once and forget about. It is something you monitor throughout your career. "In advancing a career," advises one observer of the profession, "you have to be able to recognize how each phase of a career connects to each other phase. The best way to think of a career is a little like a novel, with each chapter connecting to the other." Harry Gilbert puts the same thought a different way. "On each change of job," he said, "you should ask yourself the question, 'Will the new job prepare me for the ones that may follow?'"

CAREER PLANNING: SOME GENERAL THOUGHTS

I am going to assume that your primary career goals in accounting are twofold: you want to make enough money to give you financial security, and then some. At the same time, you want to derive a sense of fulfillment from what you are doing. To be sure, you can achieve these twofold objectives in any number of ways in accounting—as a partner in public accounting; as a chief financial officer or the chief executive officer of a corporation; as an executive accountant in government; as a public accountant in your own practice; or, finally, in a business in which you are not really working as an accountant but rather using your accounting knowledge, which, as all accountants know, is an excellent foundation for success in any business.

In my own case, early in my accounting career I recognized that while I considered myself a competent accountant and enjoyed the work, I took more pleasure in business than in accounting. But that is my decision. I know of many highly successful accountants who would never dream of leaving accounting itself. Judging by the success they have enjoyed, they have obviously made the right decisions for themselves. That is a key point: you should make the career plans that truly reflect what *you* want.

To make such decisions, you have to know yourself. You have to know what you want out of accounting, what you are willing to do in order to reach that objective, and, finally, whether you have (or can develop) the skills and personal traits required to achieve this objective.

I cannot tell you what you want and can do. I *can*, however, ask you some questions. Your answers should give you some idea, at least, of whether your career has a plan.

1. *Do you have a career plan?* Have you established a specific career goal and a general strategy for reaching that goal? If not, you run the risk of drifting from job to job without building toward anything.

2. *Is your goal a realistic one?* Have you taken the time to evaluate realistically your chances of achieving your goal? For instance, if your goal is to set up your own practice, do you have the contacts—and the money—you will need to go out on your own?

3. *Are you following your plan?* Is your present position on the career path leading to your goal? If not, is it leading to a position that will bring you closer to your goal? If you are not following your career plan, is there a logical reason?

4. *How satisfied are you with your present job?* Do you have the responsibility and are you receiving the salary you think you deserve? If not, are you in a position to do anything about it.

5. *Are you satisfied with your pattern of progress in your present company?* Relative to others in your company, how would you assess your advancement rate? If you are moving forward in your present job, your career plan is probably moving as well.

If you answered "yes" to all of the questions above, chances are that your career path is on target. Each "no" answer, on the other hand, indicates the possibility of a detour. You would do well to examine the reasons for the "no" answer and to think about what steps you might take to deal with the problem.

CAREER PLANNING: EARLY DECISIONS

Many accountants who are looking for career success have their early decisions made for them. Because being a CPA is an important credential for career advancement in both public and private firms and in many states the only way you can qualify to be certified is to get CPA firm experience, you are most likely going to start with a CPA firm. This is true whether your long-term career goals are in public accounting or in management accounting. Most of you reading this have probably long since passed this stage of your career, but some of you may still be in college, in which case the decision lies in front of you: which type of firm is best to start with—a large, well-known national firm, or a small to medium-sized local firm?

Conventional wisdom holds that if you do get recruited out of college by one of the national firms, you should consider yourself lucky and take the job, regardless of whether your career goals lie in public accounting or in management accounting. However, our Burke survey of chief financial officers and CPA partners turned up an interesting finding: Given a choice between "getting as much varied experience as possible" or "going with a big national firm," many more chief financial officers and CPA partners recommended the former.

Not that there is a clear-cut choice between the two. The larger, better known firms do offer more prestige and usually pay better *starting* salaries. Generally, too, when you are working for a very large firm—certainly at the beginning of your career—you do not have to concern yourself too much with client development, although as competition keeps heating up in accounting, even the larger firms are going to have to concern themselves more with staff assistance in client development. Finally, if you meet the requirements, you have a chance at becoming a partner somewhat faster in a large firm than in a small firm.

So much for the advantages of spending your first few years in accounting with a large public firm. There are some disadvantages as well. For example, in a larger firm you run the risk of being pigeonholed a little too early in your career. You could find yourself spending all your time in one industry or with one client. One accountant I know spent three years working on one audit for one airline. Mind you, this might have been an excellent job for this accountant, but usually accountants who become too narrowly specialized early in their careers are jeopardizing their chances for advancement later on. I know one accountant, for instance, who spent a good deal of time in his early years working on consolidations. He became a specialist in consolidations, but within a few years grew tired of the work. It took him quite a while to reroute his career.

You should bear in mind, too, that the pressure to get ahead is more intense in the larger firms than it is in the medium-sized and smaller firms. Sometimes this pressure can get in the way of your development as an accountant. It has been my observation that the accountants who get ahead in the larger public accounting firms are slightly more politically aggressive than average, and they make it a point to "play the game." I do not say this disparagingly. I do think, though, that if you have ambitions to rise in the largest CPA firms, you cannot sit back and wait to be noticed. You have to assert yourself early.

Many of the larger CPA firms are actually a conglomeration of small firms, with each partner having his or her own sphere of influence and with people permanently assigned to each partner. There is nothing wrong with this arrangement, but you should realize that if you are working with such a firm, you are not so much working with the *firm* as you are for one or several people. That puts your rise or fall in their hands. For better or for worse, they are your mentors.

The smaller and medium-sized firms do not lend themselves to the kinds of generalizations that apply to the larger firms. They vary enormously in terms of the kind of training you will get, the kind of work you will do, and the conditions under which you will work. Some firms put junior staff members in charge of small audits within a few months. Other firms are more conservative. In some firms, you will feel the pressure to bring in new business, but, usually, this will not be the case.

Overall, the main advantage of working for a relatively small firm—if the firm is a good one—is that you can learn more in a shorter period of time than you can in a larger firm. Buddy Martin, CPA, attributes his success today to the fact that he was able to spend his first three years in accounting with a small firm in which the senior partners were constantly out in the field with him. "It wasn't just accounting I learned," he says. "It was how to deal with clients and with special situations. Unfortunately, there are not that many firms today that can give a young accountant this kind of experience."

To sum up, the *size* of the firm you join when you take your first job in accounting is not nearly as important as the *quality* of the firm and the relevance of the experience you are likely to have to your long-term career goals. Make the choice carefully, for it could have far more bearing on your career success than you might imagine.

PUBLIC VERSUS MANAGEMENT ACCOUNTING

Clearly, one of the fundamental decisions an accountant who intends to stay in accounting and does not want to start a private practice must make is whether to establish a career path in public or management accounting. (There are other career paths, such as in government; but the vast majority of accountants are in either public accounting or management accounting.)

Before getting into the differences, let me make this overall observation: I know as many successful and satisfied accountants in public accounting as in management accounting. I also know dissatisfied and relatively unsuccessful accountants in both public and management accounting. In other words, neither public accounting nor management accounting has a monopoly on opportunity or job satisfaction. In the end, it is your decision as to which you are better suited for.

The Nature of the Work

During World War II, Eli Mason, CPA, spent two years as a controller in a defense plant in New York City, and Harry Gilbert, CPA, found himself a finance officer in the army. For both men, it was their first taste of private accounting.

When the war ended, Mason went back to public accounting and established the firm of Mason & Company. Says Mason, "I found public accounting more challenging than being in the same place every day and dealing with the same problems." Gilbert, however, decided to stay in private accounting. Says Gilbert:

> I had always loved public accounting, and before the war, I had no desire to leave it. Then, for the first time, I had a taste of what it was like not having to go from client to client, and for the first time I didn't have to suppress the frustration I sometimes used to feel when I was working with a client whose intelligence I didn't respect and yet who was earning 50 times what I was earning. In the army, I got a taste of what it was like to be a kingpin in an organization, and I liked it.

The question of which branch of accounting, public or private, is more interesting, enjoyable, and lucrative is an ongoing debate, and you are not going to find me taking any sides. As Eli Mason explains it, "In the end, it's all a matter of personality." It is possible, however, to make a few generalizations.

One of my observations over the years has been that public accounting is better suited to people who enjoy pure accounting per se, whereas management accounting is better suited for people who are interested more in business than they are in accounting. I have noticed, too, that private accountants, as a group, seem to prefer concentrating on one set of problems—those of the company they work for—and like to deal with the same people every day rather than service a number of different clients.

There are other differences. "Public accountants are probably a little more analytical as a rule than management accountants," says Frank Davidson. "They generally refer to the pieces once they've been put together, whereas management accountants are more interested in the day-to-day decisions that put the pieces together in the first place."

Adds Charles Wolff, "To succeed in public accounting you have to be the type who likes to sink your teeth into a project and develop it from an idea to completion."

A lot of it has to do, too, with how much you relish the pressure of the profession. There is pressure, of course, in both public and private accounting, but most people would agree that the pressure is greater in public accounting. The pressure has to do not only with the job itself—the deadlines come more frequently and you are under the gun from more sources—but also with the pressures that public accounting puts on your home life because of the travel and the long hours.

"If you're married, you need a very understanding spouse to succeed in public accounting," says Larry D. Gipple, CPA, the administrative personnel partner of McGladrey Hendrickson & Co. "We lose more good people because of marital relationships than we do from the pressure per se." Adds Don Prince, CPA, from our Pittsburgh franchise, "Some people simply can't handle the tremendous pressure and time demands of public accounting. You don't just work for a boss; you also work for a client who has unreasonable demands—some of them on weekends."

On the other hand, the pressures in management accounting are more a reflection of the company and the person you work for than the job. At their worst, the pressures you are up against in private accounting are not nearly as great as those in most public firms.

Where the Money Is

It used to be said that you could earn more money in private accounting than you could in public accounting. This may still be true at the middle levels of each, but at the entry levels, according to the *Prevailing Financial and Data Processing Starting Salaries* guide published each year by Robert Half International, Inc., accountants in large and medium-sized public firms earn, on the average, about 16 per cent *more* than internal accountants working in private industry. At the upper levels, it is safe to assume, there really is not much difference at all. The earnings of the managing partners of the largest public accounting firms are on a par with those of *Fortune* 500 CEO salaries. I also know partners in medium-sized CPA firms who, because of the deals they have had access to, have made far more money than they could have hoped to have earned in private industry; by most standards, these partners are considered quite wealthy.

If there are differences in the earning capacities of accounting positions, the factor appears to be the size of the company or firm, rather than whether you are in public or private accounting. The average corporate controller CPA with a company whose yearly volume is between $10 million and $50 million starts between $46,000 and $57,000 in 1987. Controllers starting with companies with volume in excess of $750 million, on the other hand, were earning between $110,000 and $161,000. Similar differences, though not quite as dramatic, prevail in public accounting as well.

Where there is definitely a difference between public and private accounting is in job security, for there is no question but that public accounting offers more security than private accounting. "Public accountants who are good technicians have what amounts to almost guaranteed employment," maintains Frank Bartl, CPA, who is associated with our Long Island franchise. "Public accountants can change jobs at any time because they have a trade, and there's a market out there for them as long as they can function."

The same is not true in private accounting. First of all, it is much easier for a public accountant to move into private accounting than it is for a private accountant to move into public accounting. Public firms, except in rare situations, would almost always prefer to hire someone with a career background in public accounting. Second, experience in private accounting is not as easily transferable from one job to another. If you are a management accountant with many years of experience in, say, food service companies, you are going to have trouble convincing an oil company that you are qualified for a job in that company. Third, because private accountants do not have the contacts public accountants develop, their job possibilities are more limited than those of public accountants. "Private accountants," says Buddy Martin, "don't have as wide a world to choose from as public accountants do."

Making the Move from Public to Private Accounting

Years ago, I knew a CPA—let us call him Jack—who had been associated with a major public accounting firm for more than 15 years. One day he asked me to lunch. "Bob," he told me, "I have to get out of this company. I don't like most of the people here, and they don't like me. I'm never going to make partner. What I'd really like is to get out of public accounting and become a controller in a good company."

On the surface, Jack's ambition to leave public accounting and get into management seemed reasonable enough. Thousands of public accountants make the same kind of move every year. Only one thing was wrong. When you've been in public accounting for as long as Jack had been—15 years—it is tough to land a good job in private accounting—unless, that is, you can connect with a client firm. I could have gotten Jack a job, but it would have been with a relatively small company and he would have had to take a salary cut.

As it happens, I convinced Jack to stay put, and eventually he became a partner in the firm, but he is no exception. I have met many accountants like him: accountants who have wanted to move from public to private accounting but simply waited too long to make the move. The reason I say "too late" is that the most sought-after positions in accounting—partnerships in the public firms and CFO positions in industry—are not positions you can wake up one day and decide you want. You have to plan years in advance for them.

Granted, there are exceptions. Donald H. Trautlein, chairman of Bethlehem Steel, spent 25 years at Price Waterhouse before he joined Bethlehem. However, as is almost always the case when the move to private accounting takes place after so long a period of time. Trautlein was already handling the account (Bethlehem) at Price Waterhouse. More typically, the accountants who have gone the furthest in industry have made the shift from public to private accounting fairly early in their careers. Harold S. Geneen, CPA, former chairman of International Telephone and Telegraph, left Lybrand, Ross Bros. & Montgomery (now Coopers & Lybrand) to become chief accountant for an American Can Company subsidiary in 1942, about seven years after he joined Lybrand. James L. Ketelsen, CPA, president and chief executive officer of Tenneco Inc., spent four years in public accounting before joining a Tenneco subsidiary as an assistant controller. J. Paul Lyet, CPA, chairman and chief executive officer of the Sperry Rand Corporation, spent only two years with Ernst & Ernst before joining the Sperry New Holland farm equipment division as controller.

Most successful accountants I have spoken to advise young account-

ants who want to move into corporate finance at the *Fortune* 500 level
to spend at least three or four years with a good CPA firm. By "good"
they are not necessarily talking about a large firm, but about a firm that
has more than a few major clients. I would add that, if you are
contemplating a career in private accounting, you should not stay in
public accounting for more than six or seven years.

On the other hand, an interesting—and significant—change is now
taking place in the accounting departments of many of the country's
largest corporations, as a result of which accountants who previously
might have been expected to pay some dues in the public accounting
firms before corporations would consider them are now being hired
much sooner—and are being hired into positions that offer an
excellent springboard to career advancement.

What is happening, in brief, is this: new changes in the reporting
procedures that public companies must follow have changed the
reporting lines in many corporations and, in the process, have
enhanced the responsibility and status of internal auditors. Today,
instead of reporting directly to the controller, internal auditing
departments are more likely to report to the chief financial officer and
to the audit committee—a group of "outside" directors that New York
Stock Exchange corporations trading securities must now establish and
operate.

The upshot of these changes is twofold. First, the importance of the
new role of the internal auditor, coupled with the complexity of the
function, has led many corporations to compete with the major public
accounting firms for the same top accounting majors that corporations
would not have aggressively recruited ten years ago. More important,
though, accountants who get hired into these internal auditing
positions are automatically on the "fast track," and with good reason.
Spending two years in internal audit under the new rules gives the
auditor a very good picture of the company as a whole. What is more,
because internal auditors are becoming increasingly more involved in
analytical functions (that is, determining the cost-effectiveness of
functions and operations), internal audit is no longer perceived as
simply a cost center.

It is worth mentioning, too, that more and more states are now
putting internal auditing involvement in the same category as public
accounting experience when it comes to meeting the CPA experience
requirement.

Another point worth stressing here is that, when you *do* make the
move, choose the company with care. It is understandable, once you
have been with a good public accounting firm for four or five years,

to want a position with stature and responsibility, such as a controllership, and frequently there may be a controllership available, albeit in a very small firm with no great future.

Keep in mind that successful companies will rarely put you into a controllership position directly from public accounting—unless you have already been involved with that company for many years. So, when you make your move, you have to think three or four years down the road, rather than dead-end yourself in a position that has no future. Do not hesitate to start with a good corporation as an internal auditor if the advancement opportunitities are reasonably clear. You will be able to get a good perspective of the entire operation, meet the right executives throughout the company, and subtly influence getting an attractive job transfer.

CAREER PATHING: OTHER CONSIDERATIONS

Even if you have chosen (or been chosen by) a firm that fits well into your career plan, you still have a number of decisions to make that will go a long way in determining your ultimate career success. Here are some of the considerations and what you should bear in mind about each.

THE CPA CREDENTIAL

I know of many accountants who have never become CPAs and have nonetheless done very well in accounting. Then again, these accountants represent a vanishing minority. The CPA credential has always been a useful career asset but, as our Burke study showed, virtually 100 per cent of the CPA partners and chief financial officers queried considered being a CPA "important"—and the certification is becoming increasingly important each year.

It is not only that being a CPA automatically increases your earning power (in private accounting, for instance, CPAs earn an average of 10 per cent more than non-CPAs), it is more that not being a CPA limits your career options. If you are not certified, you can almost forget about becoming a partner in a CPA firm. (You can, however, become successful as a non-CPA in a CPA firm by being a recognized expert in a specialty or by being an effective business getter.)

It is possible, of course, that you have no intention of staying in accounting, in which case you might consider sitting for the CPA exam a waste of your time. I do not agree. I still have the CPA credential, even though I have been out of accounting for more than 35 years. Being a CPA gave me a recognizable career credential.

THE CMA CREDENTIAL

As yet, the Certified Management Accountant has neither the prestige nor the numbers that the CPA license can claim. (There are a few more than 7100 CMAs today as compared with an estimate of 325,000 CPAs.) Even so, I think the CMA is an important credential that will become increasingly important in years to come, and, therefore, well worth pursuing. In Canada and England, for instance, an accountant who holds the equivalent of the United States CMA has almost as much recognition as the accountant who is a chartered accountant (CA). Chartered accountants and industrial accountants are not licensed, but their associations are very strong, and if, for some reason, an accountant is dismissed from the association, his or her career could be severely damaged.

My personal view of the CMA situation is that it should be tied into the licensing of management accountants. Management accountants, like CPAs, should have to be approved and certified by a state board, and passing the CMA exam should be a requirement. (However, all CPAs and those practicing as management accountants should be grandfathered.) I am well aware that many CPA partners do not share my viewpoint and see no reason for licensing management accountants, but more and more CPAs are at least beginning to appreciate that management accountants need more official recognition from the accounting profession.

Norman Auerbach, for instance, believes that to be "a totally professional" person, an accountant should have a strong educational base—at least five years of classes. At the conclusion of the period of study, the person could qualify as a professional accountant by passing an examination. "Thereafter," he says, "if an accountant wants to go into management and industry, he or she should work for two years and then take the CMA exam. If this accountant wants to go into public accounting after two years of CPA experience, he or she would take the CPA exam. This would offer greater professional stature to accountants, irrespective of their area of interest."

Interestingly enough, the CMA exam may be more difficult in some ways than the CPA exam because it covers a broader range of areas, among them economics, statistics, banking, and finance. Thus, passing the exam indicates to prospective employers that you have achieved a certain level of expertise. Also, as Dr. James Bulloch, managing director of the Institute of Management Accounting, points out, "Passing the CMA demonstrates to other people your commitment to further personal and business development, and you show that your interest goes beyond the narrow confines of the job you're now working in."

According to surveys taken by the Institute of Certified Management Accountants, accountants who have become CMAs have nothing but praise for the program. Of the more than 7100 accountants who have passed the examination, 97 per cent would recommend the CMA program to other accountants. Apart from their feeling that the CMA has helped advance their careers, many cited the personal challenge and feeling of satisfaction that came from passing the exam.

How important will the CMA be over the next ten years? It is difficult to say. James Bulloch estimates that in time, as the National Association of Accountants, through its Institute of Certified Management Accountants, continues to promote the CMA, there will be some 20,000 CMAs. And Edward Lutz, who has as broad a perspective of accounting as anyone, says flatly that if he had a son or daughter interested in accounting, he would recommend sitting for both the CPA and the CMA examinations. My own feeling about the CMA, which I have expressed in many articles, is that it is an achievement and a credential that is well worth a management accountant's time.

HOW MUCH SHOULD YOU SPECIALIZE?

Becoming knowledgeable in one particular specialty—taxation, for instance—can undoubtedly be useful as a career strategy. Specialists often earn more money than nonspecialists, and the reason many clients switch auditors, according to changes listed in the *Public Accounting Report,* is to get the services of a firm that specializes in their particular industry or discipline.

But if specialization can earn you a slightly higher salary and can benefit the firm you work for, it does not necessarily benefit you in the long run. It may actually limit your career options, for your appeal is limited to firms that have a need for your specialty. Yes, if you are a top specialist, it is possible to earn more than some of the partners in the firm, but what is in vogue today may not be in vogue tomorrow. Who would have guessed in the mid-1970s, for instance, that accountants who specialized in the oil and gas industry would not be in great demand in the 1980s?

HOW IMPORTANT IS THE MBA?

More and more young accountants are getting their MBAs. Our Burke survey suggests that an MBA is more important in management accounting than in public accounting. Some 82 per cent of top management personnel and 72 per cent of chief financial officers felt that an accountant with an MBA was more likely to get ahead. Only 59 per cent of CPA partners felt the same way. More significantly, roughly one out of four CPA partners queried took issue with the idea that an MBA was helpful to an accountant's career, whereas only 8 per cent of top corporate management and 15 per cent of chief financial officers saw little value in the MBA.

"I don't think an MBA is *vital*," says Peter Skomorowsky, CPA, who heads the New York office of Alexander Grant, "but it gave me a broader base of ideas than I think I would otherwise have had. I think the viewpoint instilled by the MBA program is valuable, but I'm not convinced you need to be an MBA to *have* that viewpoint."

As I see it, timing has a lot to do with the relative value of the MBA. If you can afford to get your MBA before you start to work full time, go ahead and do it. However, given a choice between concentrating full time on your first accounting job or dividing your time between work and graduate studies, you are better off devoting your energy to the job. I am not minimizing the importance of the MBA, as either a learning experience or a credential, but what will ultimately determine your success is job performance and not degrees.

GOVERNMENT

More than 100,000 accountants in the United States work for the government, many of them in agencies such as the IRS, the FBI, the SEC, and the GAO. While I have to admit that, years ago, I would have been reluctant to suggest to accountants with high career goals that they take a job with the government, I am beginning to have second thoughts, especially when it comes to jobs at the municipal level. More and more today, municipalities are switching from fund accounting to GAAP, which means that the work is much more interesting and challenging. Then, too, even though government salaries for accountants are not quite as high as salaries in the private sector, the salaries are higher than they used to be, and there is not the same degree of pressure.

TEACHING

"Upgraded accountants," noted *Business Week* in its guide to careers, "will require better educated accountants," which, in turn, bodes well for opportunities in teaching. A teaching career is hardly the target you want to set for yourself if your goal is purely to make money, but most of the accountants I know who teach would not trade places with anybody. What the accountants who do it seem to like best about teaching are, first, the academic lifestyle and, second, the process of teaching unto itself. As Dr. Henry Anderson of the University of Central Florida puts it, "You have to love students and a life that's less structured."

One thing is certain. If you have reasonable credentials and can demonstrate basic teaching ability, you should not have too much trouble finding work on many of the university campuses across the country. Given the differences in pay scale between teaching and other areas of accounting, there has always been a shortage of teachers and, given the nature of human beings, that shortage is not likely to ease very soon.

CAREER PATHING: SOME FINAL CONSIDERATIONS

Career pathing is probably the most difficult aspect of the accounting profession on which to offer specific advice. It is difficult, for one thing, to know what your ultimate goals are, and, once you establish these goals, it is no mean trick to chart and follow the path most likely to reach these goals.

If there is a key to successful career planning, it is being willing to take the time, periodically throughout your career, to reexamine your situation carefully. You continually have to ask yourself if the career goals you formulated two or three years ago are as important to you today. You have to take a hard look to determine whether you are closer today to those goals than you were when you first formulated them. You also have to be alert to any new situations that may have arisen in your job or in your firm that could have an impact on your career goals. Perhaps your career is moving in a direction that is inconsistent with what you eventually want out of accounting. Perhaps, out of necessity, you have been thrust into a role that may be benefiting the firm but is not taking you in the direction you want to go.

Above all, you need to be flexible, and you need to keep in mind that no one career path can qualify as the model. Look at James W. McKee, an accountant who is now CEO of CPC Industries and who spent most of his first seventeen years with the company in Brazil where, as he explains, the monumental inflation problems forced him to get involved in all of the financial operations of the company and to be, as he puts it, "more than just an accountant." Or, look at Southern Bell's Ed Rast, who began his career with the company as a lineman in Miami.

But, possibly, the most interesting career path I was able to uncover during my interviews was that of Dennis A. Osterdock, a CPA who ran his own consulting firm in Fairbanks, Alaska. Osterdock's original career goal was to join his father's CPA firm in Stockton, California, and so he spent his first two years out of college with Price Waterhouse, planning all along to join his father's firm within a few years. "Then I decided," he said, "to spend a year looking around before I finally settled in with my father."

During that year Osterdock applied for—and got—a job with a small land development company in Fairbanks and a year later he found himself a part owner of Alaska Airlines. Not too long afterward, Osterdock decided to go back to Stockton and work with his father, but, as he puts it, "My heart was really in Alaska." He returned to Alaska, set up a management consulting firm, and eventually went into partnership with another man in a steel fabricating company. "We ran the company together for two years," Osterdock explains, "and then we brought in an employee from Seattle to run things. That's when I started looking around for something else to do and decided that Alaska needed a good recruiting firm."

Osterdock cannot say for sure what he will be doing five years from today, but he is convinced that his willingness to move in directions he did not originally think of has not only helped to make him successful but has given him a rich and fulfilling background. His is not the classic career path, but it is not a bad one to keep in mind.

How to Handle Yourself on the Job

5

There's no such thing as not having enough time if you're doing what you want to do.

As I have been stressing all along in this book, career success in accounting depends upon qualities that go beyond technical expertise, and the further you advance in the profession, the more important these qualities become. What, exactly, *are* these other qualities—the qualities that, when combined with technical competence, differentiate successful accountants from the accountants struggling to hold their own in the middle levels?

I put this question to nearly everyone I interviewed for this book and, as you might expect, I received a variety of answers. Eli Mason, for instance, talked in terms of feeling a sense of responsibility "to your clients, to your profession, and to the public." William Kanaga talked about learning how to view problems through the eyes of the client. Bob Anderson stressed motivation, noting that almost all the accountants he has observed who have failed to achieve career potential were insufficiently motivated. William S. Wernersback, a partner in Pannell Kerr Forster, emphasized dedication and the ability to communicate: "We look for people," he says, "who can dedicate themselves and who can communicate not only with clients but within the organization as well."

Saul Silverman talked about a combination of qualities. "You need competence, compassion, and understanding," he said, "but at the same time you need a level of professional independence." Dr. Emanuel Saxe, a CPA and prominent educator, stressed, among other things, the importance of being able to think logically. "Since auditing involves the making of many important judgments," he said, "it is most important that they be based upon sound reasoning."

I was especially intrigued by the observation of Dr. Abraham J. Briloff, CPA, author of *Unaccountable Accounting, More Debits Than Credits* and *The Truth About Corporate Accounting.* Briloff talks of the qualities that distinguish accountants as a "series of interrelated I's." He talks first of "intellectual competence" and adds "independence." "The third," he says, "would be integrity, which dovetails with independence." Briloff mentions the quality of intrepidity, which he defines as the "ability or the willingness to take risks for what one considers to be desirable rather than just determining to go along because that's the way you might get along." He also talks about "pensive indignation," which means "the willingness to speak out overtly when we see wrong prevailing." Finally, in Briloff's "series of I's," there is what he calls the ultimate I—which is how each individual relates to the totality of relationships.

I can do little more than echo the views expressed by the accountants I have just mentioned. Motivation, dedication to the profession, clear thinking, a sense of responsibility to the people you work with or for, integrity, good judgment—these and others are crucial qualities for accountants seeking success. But *having* these qualities is not enough. You have to be able to demonstrate these qualities day after day on your job. In this chapter, we will look at the various ways you can do this.

BE A TEAM PLAYER

I know of no accounting firm or any corporation (of any size) that does not put a high premium on company loyalty. "It's a very positive attribute," says William Morgan of Peat Marwick Mitchell. "The fact that you're proud of your organization can't help but show itself in everything you do, particularly in your dealings with clients."

You demonstrate company loyalty in any number of different ways. The easiest—and the most important—way is to support your company policies. But there are other, subtler things that can demonstrate loyalty and pride: little things that you might not think about, like being punctual and putting in a *full* day's work; being willing, when the need arises, to work extra hours; and being pleasant and courteous to all the people you work with, from the receptionist to the head of the firm.

These are little things, but do not underestimate their importance.

Many times these qualities alone—punctuality, caring, the willingness to work hard—have induced companies to keep, and eventually promote, people they might otherwise have terminated. I can recall one situation in particular in which a not especially good accountant in a Wall Street firm was promoted to customer service because the company did not want to fire an employee who was loyal and hardworking.

By the same token, you need to develop good working relationships with the people who work both *for* you and *with* you. I will be looking into the various aspects of managing in the next chapter, but, for now, I want to stress the importance of treating *everyone* you come into contact with in your job with respect—and this goes for the entry-level people in your firm as well. One of the most successful executives I know has always made it a practice, whenever his secretary or other members of the firm's administrative staff have had to put in extra hours to finish a project, to acknowledge the extra work with a small token—a rose, for instance. "One thing I've learned in business," he says, "is that if you want people to go an extra mile for you, you need to show them how much you appreciate it."

On the other hand, I heard a story recently about a firm in which one of the accountants was so high-handed in his dealings with the data processing department that his assignments were routinely given last priority. The somewhat amusing thing about this situation is that nearly everybody else in the firm was delighted with the job the data processing department was doing, and so the complaints that this particular accountant kept making had little impact on the partners in the firm.

I am talking here about more a matter of mindset than anything else. If you recognize that, by being nice to people and by showing your appreciation in tangible ways, you are benefiting *yourself*, it will be that much easier for you to develop the rapport and gain the support you need in organizations to get ahead. I am not suggesting that you flatter people you would not normally be nice to, but something as simple as saying "Good morning" to the people you see when you arrive at work each morning can go a long way to smooth out your working relationships. The point, let me emphasize, is not to make everyone you work with think you are the greatest human being in the world. The point is to make sure that when you need help, the people you need it from will be there to offer it.

One of the most difficult things about being a team player, not only in accounting but in any job, is getting along with a boss who may not be the easiest person to deal with. Many accountants who want to make a change are looking for this very reason: they do not get along with their supervisors. But, I have noticed that many accountants who leave jobs because they do not get along with their bosses run into the same problems in their new jobs. On the other hand, when I asked one of the most successful accountants I ever met to explain his rapid rise in one of the large CPA firms, he said to me, "I always made my boss look good."

It is part of your job responsibility not only to get along with your supervisors but to make their lives easier. One way to do this is to make up your mind to do more than follow orders. In other words, do your best to *anticipate* your boss's needs. You should know, for instance, the communication style your boss prefers: whether he or she likes you to spell things out in detail or simply give the rough outline of a project. You should be able to sense when your boss is under pressure and pitch in to ease the pressure. You should also know as much as you can about the person your boss reports to and the kinds of pressure this person puts on your boss. The better you can understand these stresses, the better you will be able to anticipate them. I repeat: whatever you can do to make your boss's life easier and to make your boss look better will generally enhance your own career progress.

The last aspect of being a team player is giving your company your full time and your best effort. This is not always easy, particularly if you are pursuing an advanced degree at night, which is why I advise young accountants who are just beginning with a firm to think twice before jumping into graduate school. As I mentioned earlier, advanced degrees do give you an edge in the marketplace, but if, in the course of pursuing the degree, you reduce your contribution to your company during the day, I think you are making a mistake. "The big problem," says Alex Cohen, publisher of *The Practical Accountant*, "is simple energy. I don't care who you are. If you're going to school 2 or 3 nights a week, you simply can't give your firm the extra time when necessary. You lack flexibility."

MOONLIGHTING: YES OR NO?

The same principle applies to moonlighting. For many, the temptation to pick up extra money on the side doing tax work, write-ups, and consulting is understandable, but many public accounting firms prohibit their employees from moonlighting as accountants and frown on moonlighting in general.

This prohibition apart, the vast majority of the accountants I have seen who moonlight do not move as far in their companies as accountants who give their full-time effort to their primary job. I believe in putting all my eggs in one basket and then watching that basket.

If you decide to moonlight, two words of caution. First, do not keep it from your company and, second, do not under any circumstances link the name of your employer to your private practice. A CPA firm I worked for years ago fired a manager at the peak of the tax season because they found he was doing his own tax work on the side and, worse, was trading on his company's name with his after-hours clients.

Obviously, giving all your attention to the job you currently hold does not always pay big dividends, but that is the risk you accept when you join an organization. My feeling has always been that many accountants never really dig in and give their job everything they can. I am not talking about sacrificing every other part of your life for your job—not at all. I am talking about giving the job everything it is worth—and a little more.

SEE THE TOTALITY OF YOUR JOB

One of the themes that recurred again and again in my conversations with accountants is the importance of seeing past the numbers and, in particular, of being able to relate these numbers to overall business objectives. "The further you go in accounting," says Pat Southerland, from the District of Columbia,

> the more important your ability to look beyond the numbers you're working on becomes. If you're doing the accounts receivable section of an audit, the question you have to ask yourself is how all of this interacts with other sections. If you run into a problem, you have to see how that problem relates not only to you, but to everybody else.

Too many accountants are unable to do what Southerland talks about. They manifest what Buddy Martin calls "tunnel vision." "They don't see the whole picture from the client's point of view," says Martin. "They see only a set of numbers, and they don't relate to the people those numbers represent."

The only way to achieve the correct perspective is to broaden your business and intellectual horizons in any way you can. You should be educating yourself (assuming the courses and seminars you take do not interfere with your daily responsibilities) above and beyond the requirements of Continuing Professional Education (CPE) and beyond the requirements of the AICPA and of many states and the SEC.

If you are in public accounting, you should make it your business to learn as much as you can about each client you work with: not just how much money it earns, but the history of the company, the products it sells, and the people who run the company. As a management accountant, you should be thoroughly familiar not only with your own company, but with the industry of which it is a part. What is more, even though the continuing education requirements are not as formalized as they are in public accounting, you should still continue to educate yourself in the state of the art.

One of the best ways, apart from going to school and reading, to gain broad knowledge is to seek out someone who has been with the company a long time and to get as much information from this person as you can. In other words, find a good mentor. "Too many young accountants," says Saul Silverman,

> fail to realize what a valuable resource they have in the older members of the firm they work for. Most people who've been with a company for a long time are flattered when a younger accountant comes to them for help and information. I know that in my career when younger people have come to me for information or advice, I was only too pleased to give it, and I was always surprised when there were employees who tried to do it all alone.

KNOW WHERE THE POWER IS

I have never seen a company (or any organization, for that matter) that was not "political" to some degree—political in the sense that certain people in the organization hold power disproportionate to their position. All things considered, accounting is probably a little *less* political than other areas of business, but to say that, as an accountant, you do not have to concern yourself with company politics would be naive.

In some cases, you may find that getting ahead in your firm will be tied to your ability to emulate the style of top management. I worked for a firm once in which one of my co-workers emulated almost everything about the president of the company, from the way he walked, to facial expressions—even to the kind of cigars the boss smoked. Not surprisingly, my co-worker became the president's "fair-haired boy." (Then again, when the company was sold, guess who was one of the first to be let go?)

One of the best, if not one of the easiest, ways of gaining recognition is to take on those jobs that no one else wants to do—providing, that is, that you are doing them for the right person and providing it is the right kind of job. Taking on a boring assignment—a one-day trip to an out-of-town bank to examine one stock certificate—is likely to be unappreciated. But taking charge of the United Way campaign in your firm, while it might seem a thankless job, could gain you important recognition, especially if the chairperson of the campaign is somebody with power.

Yet another way to gain recognition is to anticipate your firm's needs, which you can do by analyzing where your firm's weaknesses may lie and by making it your business to develop strengths in these areas. Dan Kramer recalled that, in the early years of Oppenheim Appel Dixon & Co., his ability to write gave him a special niche in dealing with partners and managers.

> It got to the point where almost any correspondence that went out of the firm had to go through me first. I saw everything that went out, and people would come to me and want to know, "When did we do this or that?" I was one of the few people they could come to because I had hands-on exposure to a great deal of the accounting firm's information.

Just imagine, for example, if years ago you could have foreseen the role of computers in accounting and you had learned about computers before anybody else in the organization knew anything about them. You would not necessarily have to know how to program the computer. Simply knowing what is around and what is suitable for your company might have been enough to give you additional stature.

PROTECTING YOUR INTEGRITY

A few months after a man found a position as a chief financial officer with a medium-sized public company, the chairman of the board of that company called him in and gave him some specific instructions on how he, the chairman, wanted the financial statements to look on the next SEC quarterly report. The company, it turned out, was contemplating a merger and the chairman wanted the records to make the company's financial position look healthier than it really was. The CFO balked and the chairman gave him an ultimatum: follow orders or leave.

The CFO was in a tough bind. He was being paid well and he liked his job. But he refused to compromise his integrity and, as things turned out, he did the right thing by leaving. The company merger did, in fact, take place, but none of the key executives in the company were retained by the acquiring company, and, once the discrepancies became evident, there were also all sorts of investigations. The CFO, in the meantime, has done well for himself. We found him another job, with another company and at a higher salary. So, by protecting his integrity, he ended up protecting his own career.

LEARN HOW TO MANAGE YOUR TIME

Time is in short supply for accountants, and few skills you develop in your professional career will have more bearing on your progress than your ability to manage your time efficiently.

Most good accountants are detail oriented. But sometimes this concern for detail can get out of hand. You can spend so much time trying to resolve a 35-cent discrepancy that you overlook a $1 million error. A CPA friend of mine was complaining recently to me about an accountant who, if he is testing a month of bills for an audit and cannot find a particular invoice, immediately decides to check another 100 invoices. He said:

> What I'd like my auditors to do is to use some judgment. You have to ask yourself in a situation like this if the lost invoice is an isolated instance or indicates a possible lack of control because of a poor filing or a poor control system. The point is to take a few minutes to look at the forest rather than wasting an hour concentrating on one tree.

Most successful accountants have their individual systems of managing their time. "What I try to do," says Peat Marwick's William Morgan,

> is to implement some basic time management techniques, as opposed to trying to do everything at once. I look each day at what has to be done, and what's come in, and what should be handled in terms of client affairs. Then I try to prioritize those things and put together a realistic list of what can get accomplished that day.

I should not have to remind you to begin each of your work days with a written agenda. The agenda should list all the tasks that you need to attend to that day, ranked according to priority. Not all of these tasks are going to be equally appealing, but try to resist the temptation of postponing the unpleasant ones. "In my experience," says William S. Kanaga, former chairman of Arthur Young & Company,

> when you put off dealing with a problem, the problem only gets worse. So I make it a point, if there is a really tough problem on my desk, to deal with it immediately. Dealing with the problem

may not be something I enjoy doing, but by dealing with it, I'm able to operate more effectively.

Apart from planning your day in advance, you have to make sure that you have allotted enough time to handle each of the tasks you have set down on your agenda. If it looks as if there is too much work for you to handle, do not be afraid to admit that you cannot handle the workload. Successful people, as a rule, are not embarrassed to speak up and ask for help if they are overloaded. They are not afraid that by admitting they have too much work they are showing a weakness. Follow their example.

Finally, if you have not already done so, I strongly recommend that you maintain a time log for at least one week. Do not make it complicated. Simply keep a legal pad or a daily appointment sheet near your desk and record on it what you are working on and how long it is taking to do each phase of the task.

Once you have completed a time log for at least five days, you are ready to evaluate how efficiently you are managing your time. Record on a separate sheet of paper all the tasks you have been involved with that week and how much total time throughout the week you spent on each. Then, figure out the total amount of hours you worked that week. Now you are ready to analyze whether you are spending the bulk of your time on the most important facets of your job.

Beyond this self-audit, there are a number of specific steps you can follow to help you manage your time more efficiently. Here are some of the techniques I have found particularly useful:

1. Establish—and regularly reformulate—priorities: This is a basic principle of time management, but it is a principle that is overlooked more often than most people realize. Choose whichever "system" of indicating priorities you wish—the most common method is to give each task a number from one to four—but make sure you refer to that list two or three times a day so that you can make any adjustments that may have become necessary in the course of the day.

2. Control the phone: Whenever you are involved in any task that requires sustained concentration, discipline yourself to answer those calls that require your *immediate* attention. To keep the phone under control, either have your secretary hold all calls or go someplace—a conference room, for instance—where the phone will not ring.

3. Keep your work area organized: Get into the habit of straighten-

ing your desk two or three times a day. You would be amazed at how much time you will save by *not* having to look for papers and documents hidden somewhere under the mass of other papers and documents.

ASKING FOR A RAISE

When it comes to asking for a raise, accountants are no different from business professionals in general. They are not especially comfortable with the idea of asking their companies for more money (regardless of how justified they may be in their request), and once they decide they are going to ask for the raise, they do not really know how to go about it.

There are any number of reasons why asking for a raise is so difficult for so many people, not the least of which is the difficulty many people have in placing a value on their services. But rather than dwell on these reasons, let us look briefly at some of the points to keep in mind when you decide to seek a raise.

1. *Prepare a strong case:* Before going into any salary discussion, make sure you have prepared a case that argues strongly for your raise request. The case should be built around your *accomplishments* in the company and not your personal financial needs.

2. *Know what you are worth:* Knowing how much the competition— and your own company—pays accountants with experience, ability, and seniority similar to yours should give you a rough idea of how much you are worth to your company and serve as the basis of your negotiations.

3. *Know when to ask:* The best time to seek a salary increase (periodic salary reviews notwithstanding) is shortly after you have successfully completed an important project that has benefited the company. The worst time to seek a salary increase, on the other hand, is when the company is going through a difficult time.

4. *Be flexible:* You should always go into a salary discussion with two figures in mind: (1) what you'd like, and (2) what you will settle for. Regardless of how justified you feel your request to be, never hand down an ultimatum.

HANDLING STRESS

Stress is inherent in most occupations, and accounting is certainly no exception. Nearly everything accountants do embodies a deadline of one kind or another: from a corporate client, from the government, from a supervisor. "And it's not so much the deadline itself," says Robert McCall, a CPA who owns our New Orleans office. "It's the fact that most people who are not accountants themselves simply cannot understand the kind of deadline pressure you're under. They're looking for figures, but what they don't realize is the sequence you need to go through in order to get the figures."

Some of the stress that is so much a part of accounting is, of course, necessary. "If we never felt stress in our day-to-day responsibilities," says William Kanaga, "it would mean that we were unaffected by the problems of our clients and that we'd probably lose them. It would mean that we didn't have a real and abiding interest in their problems." I think it is true, too, as Kanaga observes, that there is a weeding out process of a sort in public accounting. The accountants who cannot deal with the pressure tend to leave public accounting relatively early in their careers.

Granting that stress, in small degrees, can make you a better accountant and granting, too, that most accountants who do not deal well with stress usually end up in less stressful positions, stress remains a major problem in accounting—so much so that the AICPA has begun to offer seminars that address the problem as it applies not only to individual accountants but also to their spouses.

Few people, I think, appreciate and understand the extent of the problem of stress in accounting more than Ken Macjen (pronounced MA-son), who directs the personnel assistance program for Ernst & Whinney. This program, which was started in 1977, is designed to help the firm's accountants work through some of the stress-related problems that public accounting can often produce. "I had some personal problems of my own that had to do with stress," says Macjen. "And once I was able to solve them, with a lot of help from others, I decided I wanted to do what I could to help other people."

Macjen spends the bulk of his time counseling both accountants and their spouses. The reason he spends so much time with spouses, he explains, is that of all the stress-related problems that could affect accountants—such as alcohol, drugs, and personal relationships—the most common are marital problems.

"The problems are the most severe," Macjen says, "in those situations in which their spouses are unable to accept how difficult it is for CPAs in public accounting to meet the demands of their firm, their clients, and their families, not to mention the demands they make on themselves." He adds: "The best marriages that include a CPA are those in which the spouses understand and accept that they may not *always* come first and also recognize that it's the quality, not the quantity, of the time that's important.''

While conceding that some marital problems are difficult to avoid, Macjen maintains that many accountants compound their marital problems by putting added pressure on themselves. "What it comes down to in many marriages," he says, "is that many accountants are unable to separate what they do at the office from what they do at home.''

To illustrate his point, Macjen tells of a woman he once spoke to at one of the meetings he holds periodically with the spouses of CPAs. Her CPA husband, according to the woman, traveled frequently, and whenever he would leave for a trip at the beginning of a week, he would give his wife a yellow pad that had a "do" list on it. The pad listed a beginning cash balance. The wife was expected during the week not only to complete all the "do's" but also to keep a running balance of all expenditures. "The first thing my husband always does when he comes home at the end of the week," she said, "is to check off the 'do' list, and then make sure that the balance is correct. I get even with him, though. I'll lose a receipt on purpose, and this drives him out of his mind.''

Macjen admits that this accountant's behavior is extreme, but he says that the syndrome typified by this person is by no means a rarity among accountants. "It's what psychologists call the 'perfectionist' syndrome," he says. "Accountants are not the only professionals affected by it, but it's more common in accounting than most people think.''

The most frequent symptom of this syndrome, according to Macjen, is the inability to leave the job behind at the office. "Many accountants are so concerned with doing a good job," he says, "that they neglect every other aspect of their lives. When they're home, they're sitting in the den, talking to clients on the phone. They'll go on vacation, but they'll take work with them.''

The problem with this approach to work, says Macjen, is that it is usually self-perpetuating. "What happens," he says, "is that problems occur at home, and the accountants, because they don't know how to deal with them, will throw themselves into their work all the more. Many become workaholics.''

Ken Macjen feels that the only way many accountants can avoid this perfectionist syndrome is not to become so tied up in their careers that being a CPA is their only identity. "It isn't easy," he admits. "Many accountants have a tendency to internalize everything. They don't confront. And, too often, they're simply not willing to recognize that by pouring every bit of their energy into their jobs, they're really running away from personal problems."

It is to Ernst & Whinney's credit that they have a man like Ken Macjen doing personnel assistance work. More and more firms have begun to recognize that stress, when it gets out of hand, benefits no one. The result, in many cases, is the phenomenon referred to as "burnout." You've heard the term, I am sure. It was apparently coined by Dr. Herbert J. Freudenberger, of New York, whose early studies found a correlation between burnout and certain physiologiacl symptoms, such as constant headaches and the inability to shake colds.

"Burnout occurs," says Dr. Harry Levinson, an industrial psychologist who has specialized in this area of stress, "when a person is unable to continue what he or she is doing. People who've burned out have to throw in the sponge. They've lost energy and commitment. They've shot their wad on a particular task."

I can tell you both from observation and from conversations I have had with hundreds of accountants that burnout is not at all uncommon in accounting. Says Marc Silbert, who heads our New York franchise, "The curious thing is that the accountants who are potential candidates for burnout are often excellent job candidates. Burnout is more common among overachievers than among people who coast."

The worst thing about burnout, according to psychologists who have studied the condition, is that you can be a victim without being aware of it until the condition is well advanced. That is why specialists like Dr. Levinson insist that probably the only way to combat burnout is to be sensitive to its early symptoms—symptoms that are frequently dismissed as temporary. Here are the symptoms:

> A feeling that no matter how hard you are working, you are not getting anywhere
>
> Apathy toward nonbusiness-related tasks you once enjoyed (such as golf, tennis, music, getting together with friends)
>
> Chronic fatigue
>
> Irritability
>
> A sense of being besieged

Mind you, it is not at all unusual for accountants to experience some of these symptoms on occasion, particularly during very busy periods. But when these symptoms linger for weeks at a time, you should be concerned. When you find that your accounting work is the first thing you think about when you get up in the morning and the last thing you think about when you go to sleep at night, you are in trouble.

Bear in mind, too, that burnout is not a weakness. On the contrary, the accountants who are most susceptible to it are people who are highly energetic and have a great capacity for work. What do you do about it? Here are some suggestions from the experts:

Recognize that burnout is a problem and that if you do not attend to it, it could seriously affect your health

If the problem is serious, schedule a reasonably long vacation as soon as you can manage it

Regardless of how busy you are, do not schedule any work for the weekend and do what you can to limit the work you do at night

See what you can do about restructuring your work responsibilities—if you need help, do not be embarrassed to ask for it

Pace yourself differently throughout the day—take frequent breaks, even if it's a five-minute walk around the floor to break the tension.

HANDLING STRESS: SOME PRACTICAL ADVICE

Not surprisingly, most successful accountants have figured out a way to manage the stress in their day-to-day lives. The observations of Peat Marwick Main's William Aiken might be helpful to you. Aiken is convinced that the key to dealing with the stress of accounting is, first of all, being able to identify when you are in a situation that is more stressful than the norm. "With me," he says, "it's the fact that I'm perspiring more than usual. With other people, it might be that their heart is beating faster. But whatever the sign, I recognize it, and than I make every effort to remain as calm as I can."

When Aiken feels himself becoming unusually stressed, he takes a number of practical steps. Sometimes he will close the door and tell his secretary to hold all calls. "With the door open," he says, "the sense of a stressful environment intensifies. With the door closed, I feel a greater sense of tranquility." Another thing William Aiken does in times of stress is to find a different place to work. "I'll take what I'm working on," he says, "and go into a conference room. It's amazing what the change in environment can do to relax you."

Still another device that Aiken and other accountants I know rely on to minimize stress is to narrow the focus of their task. "I find that if I can clear my desk of everything except the project I'm working on," Aiken says, "I don't feel as flooded and I can think more clearly."

There are any number of other ways to minimize the effects of stress. For instance, I would urge you, even if you're extremely busy, not to have lunch brought into your office. Get away from the scene of the stress. Also, try to limit—and I know it's difficult—the amount of work you take home with you. Putting in four or five extra hours at home is understandable on occasion, but a steady diet of it can only wear you down in the long run.

This brings us, finally, to what may well be the most effective antidote to stress: your family and your co-workers. When Ken Macjen counsels accountants who are having problems, he emphasizes over and over the need to accept limitations and to shed the notion that asking for help is an admission of weakness. William Kanaga adds, "At Arthur Young none of the partners hesitates to ask for help when the need is there. You get brownie points for doing this."

KEEPING A PERSONNEL FILE

Whatever your specialty, you should be keeping your own **personnel file.** The file should contain a running record of every assignment, with the names and descriptions of the clients and the names of those with whom you had contact. The key point to bear in mind about this material is that it should highlight your accomplishments. Needless to say, the file should never include confidential or sensitive information.

Such a file will serve you well in several ways. To begin with, when the time comes for a salary review, you are in a position to present a strong case on your behalf—a case based on accomplishment. Second, such a file becomes invaluable should you decide to leave the firm. Your résumé will be much easier to put together and you will have strong and complete facts to present to potential employers.

SOME FINAL THOUGHTS

As I mentioned early in this chapter, doing your job well is not enough to assure you of rapid progress in your firm. Equally important is making sure that management perceives you as a valuable member of the company. In this chapter we have covered some of the ways in which you can do this. Here is a summary of the points:

1.   Show loyalty to the firm
2.   See the totality of your job
3.   Understand and anticipate your boss's needs
4.   Take credit (modestly) for your work

5. Give co-workers and subordinates the same respect you give your supervisors
6. Get recognition by taking on certain assignments nobody else will take
7. Manage your time efficiently
8. Be aware of—and take steps to counteract—job-related stress

Becoming a Better Manager

6

> The biggest failure of
> management is the failure to
> know what's going on.

It is no secret that management skills are not as highly developed in accounting as they are in many other occupations. The Burke study, for instance, found that 50 per cent of top corporate management personnel and 37 per cent of CPA partners felt that accountants are weak in managerial skills. These statistics are backed up by a study by Ralph L. Benke, a professor of accounting and director of the Center for Research in Accounting at James Madison University, Harrisonburg, Virginia.

Benke found that professionals do not leave CPA firms for more money, but for other reasons—chief of which is dissatisfaction with supervision. "Audit managers who leave," says Benke, "claim that partners are hard to please, don't praise good work, are not tactful, don't supervise enough, and are never around when they're needed." Interestingly, Benke found that the ability of the partners was rarely at issue. What was lacking, according to the terminating CPAs, was their ability to manage.

"There's not getting away from it." says Dr. Emanuel Saxe

> If you want to move to the top levels of the profession, and especially if you're looking to be a partner in one of the top firms, you have to be able to handle a large group of people intelligently

and diplomatically. To be a partner, remember, you have to be chosen.

There can be no arguing the fact that if you can manage well and have a reasonable level of technical competence, you will go much further in most accounting job situations than you would if you had strong technical skills but were weak in management skills. When the partners of the major CPA firms are considering new partners, the qualities they now look for more than any other are the precise qualities that make for effective managing: the ability to get along well with people and the ability to *motivate* people. Observes Robert Palmer, CPA, publisher of the *Public Accounting Report,* "The most successful accountants I know are those who are technically competent but have been able to drop the characteristics of the technician and have been able to pick up the characteristics of a manager of people and a manager of events."

THE ESSENCE OF MANAGING

Probably the hardest thing for most accountants who move into a managerial position to accept is the fact they are now members of management and that their role goes beyond accumulating, recording, and auditing data. The manager's job is much more people-oriented than before and calls for a new set of skills—skills most people do not come by naturally and most accountants have never mastered. Let us look into some of these management skills.

HIRING SMART

What holds true for baseball also holds true for accounting. Successful managing begins with surrounding yourself with the best possible talent—which is not necessarily the most expensive talent. From what I have observed, money usually is not the main problem when it comes to hiring the right people. The problem is that too few people know how to pick and develop talent. Our Burke marketing studies show that personnel departments rarely do the actual hiring. Except for lower salary-level jobs, you can expect, as a manager, to be doing your share of hiring. Therefore, it is important for you to sharpen your skills in picking the right people.

It is not easy to choose good people, and accountants are not the only professionals who have trouble when it comes to hiring the best people. Inefficient hiring practices are a universal problem in business today—so much so that among the most sought-after management training programs are those that teach interviewing techniques.

The Basics of Smart Hiring

Apart from the obvious—hiring the best people—two principles should govern your hiring practices. The first is always to hire with an eye toward your *total* staff and how they will work together. In other words, having an entire staff of extremely talented people might not produce good results if the chemistry is not right.

The second, and perhaps more important, principle is not to be afraid to hire someone better than yourself. Keep in mind that the better your staff members perform, the better you look. Your best people, far from endangering your job, will help you get ahead because you will be judged as someone who knows how to get the most out of your people. Let us look at some of the elements that will help you improve your skills at picking the right people.

Setting up a Recruiting "Campaign"

As I suggested earlier, your own job effectiveness is directly related to the quality of the people who work for you. As long as you keep this principle in mind, you can appreciate my view that whatever time and effort you put into hiring good people will always pay dividends in the long run.

In my book *Robert Half on Hiring* I discussed many different ways to orchestrate your own recruiting campaign. They range from looking within your own company for top candidates to placing ads in newspapers to seeking the help of outside recruiting agencies. Whichever route you go, though, let me stress one point, above all: that you stay *actively* involved with the process. If you are going to put an ad in a newspaper, you should either write the ad yourself or at least approve the copy before it goes to press. If the personnel department of your firm is going to be recruiting and screening candidates for you, you should set aside enough time to communicate your needs to the person you will be working with. The same holds true if you are using an outside personnel recruiter. It is particularly important, once you begin interviewing candidates, that you give enough feedback after each interview to give the personnel professional you are working with an increasingly clearer idea of what sort of person you are looking for.

Developing Selection Criteria

When someone you have hired fails to work out, the tendency is to blame your own judgment. You figure that if you had been a better "judge of character," you would have recognized during the employment interview that this particular candidate was not right for the job.

It may surprise you to learn that most hiring mistakes are rooted in decisions you make and steps you take long before you begin to conduct interviews. The stage of the hiring process I am talking about here is the stage at which you determine what sort of a person is really needed for the job opening.

Never underestimate the difficulty of this task. Time and again throughout my career I have found that accountants seeking to hire staff members spend little or no time analyzing the job that needs to be filled. Even when somebody takes the time to write out a job description, all too often, that description either omits key job functions or else fails adequately to reflect what the job truly demands.

There is only one way to avoid this common pitfall in hiring—that is to assume responsibility yourself for drawing up the job description and for establishing the criteria on which you intend to base your hiring decision. This is not to say that you do not seek input from other people. By all means, gather as much information as you can. Keep in mind, though, that you are the one who has to "live" with the person you hire, and you are the one who stands to lose the most if the person you hire does not work out.

Writing Out the Job Description

Take the time to really *think* about what you need and you should have no trouble coming up with a job description that can serve as the basis of your hiring campaign.

As far as specific procedures go, I suggest you keep things as simple as possible. The best way to begin is simply to list all the duties and responsibilities that you think the job you are seeking to fill requires, not worrying at first about their priority. Try to be as *specific* as you can when you are compiling this list. Instead of writing down "administrative" duties, for instance, list the actual tasks you are expecting the person you hire to perform.

After you have completed this list, you are ready to prioritize it. Here, again, keep it simple. Look at each task on your list and decide on its relative importance to the overall job function: very important, important, or not so important.

Once you have divided your list into three categories, you are ready to take a closer look at your expectations and, more important, to determine how realistic they are.

There are two key questions you need to ask yourself. First, is the job, as you have described it, genuinely *do-able.* For example, if you are expecting the person you hire to perform a great deal of detailed analysis, including economic projections and financial statements, is that person also going to have time to get involved with, say, supervision or with client relations? It is important, particularly at this stage in the hiring process, that you not take anything for granted. One of the things I used to do when I was helping clients develop realistic job descriptions was to have them estimate the number of hours per week it would take adequately to handle each of the functions listed on the job description. You would be surprised at the number of times we ended up with an 80-hour week.

Once you are satisfied that the description you have drawn up represents a *do-able* job, you are ready to ask yourself yet another question: how attractive is this job likely to be to prospective candidates?

To answer this question, of course, you need to consider not only such job-related factors as salary, benefits, conditions, and opportunity, but also the general reputation of your firm. Generally speaking, the higher the status your company enjoys, the more attractive job openings are likely to be to prospective candidates. But if your company is *not* especially well known, or if it is known for having an unusually high turnover rate, you may need to raise the offering salary or lower your standards.

What it comes down to, in the end, is recognizing the "marketability" of the job you are offering, that is, the market of candidates who not only can perform the job but will be willing to do it, but more important—willing to do it in your company.

How to Read a Résumé

If you are preparing to hire somebody, you are going to be reading dozens (maybe hundreds) of résumés, and you may use the résumés as a means of narrowing down the candidates you interview. Assuming you want to do the screening without professional assistance, there is nothing wrong with this practice. How else, after all, are you going to narrow down a long list of job candidates? What concerns me, though, is that a résumé is not necessarily a reflection of the accountant. I have seen some of the best résumé come from accountants I would have hesitated to recommend, and some mediocre résumés come from excellent candidates.

The fact is that the best résumés often come from job-jumpers, because they have the most experience writing résumés. The best way to get around this problem is to follow the example of astute clients of professional services that prefer to get their first look at the candidate and the résumé at the same time. In that way, the possibility of false impressions based on résumés is eliminated.

However, somewhere along the line you will probably see the résumé, and it can still serve you well, providing you know what to look for. For instance, you should be wary of the following:

A functional résumé: A functional résumé is one that is not organized in the usual chronological form. Frequently, this kind of résumé is used by an accountant who has a reason for not showing dates of employment. (He or she might be an excessive job-jumper.)

Excessive trivia: A résumé heavy with hobbies and interests usually denotes weakness in experience and skills.

A bitter tone: Signs of bitterness toward former employers can signal chronic discontent.

Sloppiness: A carelessly written résumé could indicate that it was prepared by an accountant with careless work habits.

So much for what you should be wary of. Here's what to look for:

Willingness to work hard: That trait is not easy to detect on a résumé, but you may be able to discern this quality by noting the accomplishments that went beyond the basics of the job.

Profit-mindedness and efficiency: Look for comments in the résumé in which the accountant mentions efficiency measures that helped increase earnings or helped improved the quality of the organization.

One other suggestion about reading a résumé—start at the end. The reason is that most candidates put the least flattering information at the end of the résumé. By reading from the end forward, you may be able to save yourself some time.

Handling the Job Interview

It goes without saying that you should never hire anybody who will work directly with you unless you yourself conduct an interview. The problem, though, is that most accountants I have known are not particularly skilled at handling the job interview. If you use an applicant rating form like the one in Exhibit 1, you will be able to compare candidates more effectively.

"My advice to interviewers," says Philip Chenok, past president of the AICPA, "is to look for the candidate's interest in the job. I was always concerned more with the questions candidates asked than I was with their answers to my question. I always tried to get a picture of the person's mind in action."

The questions a candidate asks do indeed give you a good glimpse into that candidate's mind, but you still have to control the interview. If there is any single key to gaining this control, it is your ability to get the most mileage out of each question you ask. Here are eight questions that are particularly good because they get candidates to reveal important characteristics without necessarily being aware of what they are making known:

1. *Why are you giving up your current job?* Be wary of accountants who bad-mouth their former employers. Remember, they could be malcontents and do the same thing to you a year or two down the road.

2. *What did you like best about your last job?* Candidates who cannot give you a thoughtful answer to this question probably cannot think beyond the mechanics of the job. They may lack depth.

3. *If you could have made improvements in your last job, what would you have done?* The answer to this question is a good reflection of creativity and sensitivity.

4. *Who was the most interesting client you had in your last job (or what was the most interesting job or project you've had so far in your career)?* The answer to this question will give you an idea of whether the candidate likes challenges and is perceptive.

5. *How would you describe the best person who ever worked for you or with you?* An accountant who has trouble answering this question could lack compassion.

6. *What kind of people annoy you the most?* Frequently, the traits mentioned by candidates *do not* apply to the candidates themselves.

7. *Can you describe some emergencies in some of your recent jobs in which you had to reschedule your time?* This is the question you ask instead of, "Are you willing to work extra hours when the situation calls for it?"

8. *In what way would you like our company to assist you if you join us?* Look for balance here, Be wary of accountants who indicate theymay need a great deal of help and also of accountants who suggest that they may not want any help.

You can, of course, vary these questions in any number of ways, and not all of them may be appropriate for each interview. But I like them

APPLICANT RATING

NAME _____ COLLEGE OR UNIVERSITY _____

ADDRESS _____

DATE INTERVIEWED _____ BY _____ OFFICE _____

PERSONAL GROOMING	Unkempt: Noticeable lack of neatness 1	No special care in dress or appearance 2	Neat and clean 3	Pays special attention to personal details 4	Immaculately dressed and groomed 5
PERSONAL MANNER	Nervous. embarrassed: compulsive mannerisms 1	Stiff. uncomfortable. ill at ease 2	No unusual tension. comfortable, at ease 3	Appears alert, free of tension 4	Unusually self-possessed and composed 5
EXPRESSION OF IDEAS	Unclear, illogical; speaks without thinking 1	Dwells on nonessentials; thoughts not well defined or expressed 2	Thoughts clearly expressed; words convey meaning 3	Convincing; thoughts developed logically 4	Unusual ability to express ideas logically 5
CONFIDENCE	Shy, retiring; arrogant, "cocky" 1	Submissive; argumentative 2	Reasonably self-assured. forthright 3	Shows self-confidence 4	Unusually self-assured; inspires confidence 5
MOTIVATION AND AMBITION	No drive, ambition limited 1	Little interest in development: seems satisfied 2	Interest and ambition fair; reasonable desire to work and develop 3	Definite future goals: wants to succeed and grow 4	Ambitions high, future well planned; evidence of personal development 5
EXPERIENCE AND EDUCATION	Education and experience unsuitable for the job 1	Education and experience not directly applicable 2	Good educational and work background; experience fair 3	Education and experience good: above average qualifications 4	Background especially well suited 5

Total _____

Location Preference
_____
_____

Military Obligation
Grade Point Average

Accounting _____
Overall _____

Rank in Class _____
Rank in Business School _____
Subjects of Most Interest, Other Than Accounting

Last Two Semesters

Accounting _____
Overall _____

Overall Appraisal and Comments
_____
_____
_____

REQUIRED THAT YOU CHECK ONE OF THE BOXES BELOW

Recommended and Classified by Me as—

A—☐ Outstanding
B—☐ Above Average

C—☐ Average
D—☐ Not Recommended

Signed _____ Date _____

500-12

Form 542.00[1]

EXHIBIT 1. Applicant Rating Form. [Reprinted with permission from Pannell Kerr Forster's *Personnel Management Policies and Procedures.*]

because the answers tell you a great deal about the candidate. Here is one additional word of advice: try to be as relaxed and as conversational as possible when you ask these questions. In other words, do not conduct the interview as if it were an interrogation. Your objective is not to get the best of the candidate. It is to single out the one candidate who is best for the job.

Ending the Interview

Most job interviews drag on too long—past the point at which you have all the information you need to make a decision. The reason they drag on is that many people do not know how to end them gracefully. Actually, ending an interview is not hard at all if you follow a few simple steps.

First of all, always set a time limit at the beginning of the interview and always let the candidate know at the start when the interview must come to an end. In most cases, a half-hour should be sufficient. Second, you should give clues to the candidate that will suggest the interview is nearing its end. For instance, if you are using a pencil or pen, put it aside. If you wear glasses for reading only, take them off and put them away.

But whichever way you choose to end the interview, be sure to do it on the appropriate note—appropriate, that is, with respect to how good the candidate appears to you. If the candidate is somebody you definitely want, make sure the person knows you are actively interested. If the person is a "maybe," say that you are interested but that you want time to think it over. If the person is a definite "no," be polite but noncommittal. "You have a fine record," you might say, "but I have other people to see. I'll let you know if we're interested." Whatever you do, do not say anything that might provoke a confrontation.

How to Handle References

It takes time and energy to follow through on a reference, but it is time and energy well spent—provided that you go about the process in the proper way. To begin with, you can all but ignore written references handed directly to you by the candidate. Such references are often written on the day of termination and could well reflect more guilt than accuracy. Second, see if you can get references from people who were not mentioned by the candidate; while you are talking to a person listed as a reference, see if you can get still other names of people who know the candidate.

I would also recommend that you check your references by phone instead of by mail, because many people are reluctant to put derogatory remarks down on paper. Finally, if the position you are filling is important enough, it is not a bad idea to make a personal visit to the person giving the reference. People are usually more candid when you are face to face with them than they are over the phone or in a letter.

Getting the Person You Want

It is one thing to find somebody you would like to hire but something else again to land that candidate, especially if the applicant is a coveted prospect. The better the candidates, the more likely they are to be in demand, so when you have an opportunity to hire good people, take action. Here are four guidelines:

1. *Don't delay the offer:* If a candidate is right for the job, do not hesitate to make an offer. You can always hire someone *contingent* on his or her references checking out.

2. *Limit the number of decision makers:* The more people involved in the hiring decision, the longer it will take to hire and the greater the chances the person you eventually choose will be a compromise candidate.

3. *Set an early starting date:* The longer the time between the job offer and the starting date, the greater the risk of losing a good prospect. Losing a good prospect because of a delay happens more often than you might think. You think you have "hired" somebody, but, before the person starts, another company comes along and makes a better offer.

4. *Don't fall into the "first one interviewed" trap:* Our studies show that the first person interviewed frequently does not get the job, even when that person may be the most qualified. Don't let this quirk cost you a good employee.

GETTING THE MOST OUT OF YOUR PEOPLE

Hiring the best people is one thing. Getting the most out of them is something else again. As any good manager knows, getting the most out of the people who work for you is almost a job unto itself and represents your most important managerial function. As I mentioned earlier, the very essence of managing is being able to handle people.

Robert Maynard, CPA, a partner and a national director of human resources for Price Waterhouse, attributes much of the success he has enjoyed to the fact that early in his career he was "well managed." "I remember a supervisor I had," he says, who sat down with me one day and spelled out what I was doing right and what I was doing wrong. I can remember being upset, at first, about his criticisms, but once I stopped to think about it, I realized he was right, and I accepted the fact that I had to do something about my weaknesses. This was the first truly effective counseling I'd ever received, and it made a huge difference in my career.

Robert Maynard was fortunate. He had a manager who understood that there is more to managing than making sure that tasks are completed. He worked for a manager who cared enough about Maynard to criticize him constructively, a manager, in short, who understood that the key to managing is knowing how to get along with people. Let us look at some of the specific "people skills" that are basic to successful managing.

First, get to know your people: To manage well, you need to know your staff members well. You need to be sensitive to their personality characteristics, their work patterns, and their career aspirations. You need to know—or to have a good idea of—which of your staff members are motivated primarily by financial gain and which of them are motivated by more internalized goals. You need to know how well each of them works under pressure and how sensitive each one is to criticism. More important, you need to be able to use this knowledge so that you can customize the way you handle each member of your staff.

The best way to get this information is to be alert to it. You should be aware, for instance, of how each staff member interacts with the rest of the staff. You should also make it a point, as much you can, to meet one on one with staff members (assuming you are not supervising hundreds of people) so that you can find out directly from them what their feelings are about their jobs and how you might help them improve on the job. These talks can—and should—be informal, and should not exclude any staff members. Having these talks with only part of your staff will convey the impression of favoritism.

Second, set tangible goals: If you do not tell the people who work under you exactly what you expect from them, you are committing one of the cardinal sins of managing, and you will pay for it in different ways. Those of your staff members who lack initiative will stagnate and produce very little. Those who are creative and energetic will set their goals on the basis of their own personal objectives. In both instances, the productivity in your department will suffer.

There is more to setting tangible goals than meets the eye. For instance, the tendency among most managers is to assume that the staff member understands the goal and understands the rationale behind it. Both assumptions will get you into trouble, which is why I have always felt that, when it comes to spelling out what you want, you can never be *too* specific. Far from resenting you for being so specific, most of your staff members will be grateful to be working for somebody who knows what he or she is looking for.

Third, learn how to delegate: Delegating does not come naturally. You have to learn how to do it, and the learning process, for some people, takes years. Accountants I have observed who have trouble delegating fall into one of two extremes: those who *over*delegate and those who *under*delegate. Overdelegators delegate tasks that go beyond the capability of their staff members. Underdelegators are simply afraid to let go the reins.

The many discussions I have had with accountants about delegating have convinced me that probably the most crucial factor in delegating is confidence: in yourself and in your staff. If you lack confidence in yourself, you will not be able to accept the fact that you cannot do everything yourself. You will worry that, in the event there is a mistake, you may not be able to survive it. If you lack confidence in your staff members, you will not delegate for fear that the job will not get done. There is not much I can tell you if your reason for not delegating is lack of confidence in yourself. If you lack confidence in your staff, it is clear that you have not hired the right people, so your problem has less to do with delegating than it does with choosing the right staff.

An excellent exercise for accountants who want to improve their ability to delegate is to take a pad and list all the tasks that you now perform during a typical week. Once you have done this, examine each task and ask yourself if it is a task that only *you* can perform. If this is not the case, ask yourself why you are not delegating it.

I ought to stress, too, because it is so fundamental, that delegating involves far more than dropping a job in somebody's lap and expecting it to be done to your specifications. Depending on the nature of the work and the person to whom you are delegating it, you may have to spend some time explaining exactly what you want done, and you may have to nurse the person through the first phases of the job. Many accountants lack the patience to do this. As a result, they try for a while to delegate and then, when the results are not satisfactory, go back to trying to do everything themselves.

"A good manager," says Don Prince, from our Pittsburgh franchise, "doesn't just give orders but always explains the logic behind the orders." The intelligent manager, in other words, invests the time in order to be able to delegate *more* as the staff member becomes increasingly knowledgeable and competent.

One last observation about delegating. You need to be flexible. The ability of a staff member to assume responsibility will vary not only according to that staff member's level of skill or knowledge but also according to the task itself. You have to vary your strategy from job to job. In other words, when you delegate, you have to consider both the person and the assignment.

Fourth, praise staff members for jobs well done: Praise is the most inexpensive way to motivate staff members, so do not be stingy with it. Do not praise when it is not called for; on the other hand, if you do not let your staff members know when they have done a good job, you are failing in a crucial aspect of leadership.

Many accountants are uncomfortable giving praise, possibly because they themselves worked for superiors who were not particularly generous with their praise. Yet, once you begin praising, it will become easier and easier. Eventually, it will be almost second nature.

Some advice on giving praise:

1. *Be as specific as possible:* Instead of saying, "Great job," add something specific about the project that was good. "I particularly liked the way you handled the overview section."

2. *Do not do it grudgingly:* If you are going to praise somebody, make it count. You might want to call the person into the office to do it. Another nice touch is to send a short note, even if you see the person every day.

3. *Be sincere:* Your staff members will be sensitive not only to the praise you give them, but also to the tone you use in giving the praise.

4. *Let others know about it:* When a member of your staff passes the CPA examination, for example, let the rest of your staff know about it. If a staff member gets an article published, make sure the article gets circulated among your staff, clients, or customers —if appropriate.

5. *Give tangible rewards:* Good work should be rewarded not only with praise but also with something the staff member will value. Obviously, you cannot keep giving raises every time someone does a good job, but there are nonmonetary ways of rewarding a job well done. If it is consistent with company policy, you might give somebody a day off. And, do not ignore the importance of appropriate titles, such as cost accounting specialist or retail

audit manager. Some talented accountants leave public and management accounting for a position that gives them a more impressive title. I have found that staff personnel withsuitable titles are likely to be more satisfied with their firms than those without titles.

Finally, criticize constructively: The motivating power of the praise you give your staff members will be even greater if you are also able, when necessary, to give solid *constructive* criticism. To ignore it when one of your staff members is not performing well is to do both of you a disservice. Most surveys show that employees welcome criticism, if they perceive that the criticism is fair and has the firm's and the employees' best interests at heart. When the time comes to criticize, be sure you do it in private. If at all possible, try to preface any criticism with a few words of praise.

DON'T AGONIZE OVER DECISIONS

One of the skills that good managers are supposed to have is the ability to make good decisions. Yet, as industrial psychologist Stephen Temlock points out, "If you're managing well, you don't make all that many decisions. You're mainly monitoring the decisions of others."

The point bears repeating. I know of many accountants for whom decision making is the most agonizing part of their job, and, in many cases, the decisions are not decisions they should be concerned with in the first place. Says Temlock, "If you're making too many decisions yourself, it means you don't have the right people or you don't have confidence in those people."

As a manager, you cannot ignore decision making, but it is worth pointing out that experienced managers worry far less about decision making than novice managers. "One of the skills that many executives never learn," says Irving S. Shapiro, the retired chairman of DuPont, "is when *not* to make a decision." Shapiro feels that managers will very often make a decision prematurely, without adequate facts. "What most people don't realize," he says, "is that every time you make a decision you run about a 50-50 risk of making the wrong decision. There isn't a business person around who doesn't look back at the end of each day and wonder how he survived."

One well-known accountant who developed a reputation for effective decision making was ITT's Harold Geneen. According to financial expert Felix Rohatyn, who worked for many years under Geneen and who was profiled in the January 24, 1983, issue of *The New Yorker*, Geneen had a cardinal rule about decision making. Said Rohatyn:

Geneen's rule was that if you wait to make an important decision until all the information that you might want is in, you will never make it in time. Depending on the risks, on what the stakes are, you have to settle for 75, 70, or 65 percent of the information that you need, and, on the basis of what you have, make your decision and go, because the time and the cost of getting, say, the last 25 percent are not commensurate with what you gain from deferring the decision.

The overall point here is not to let the decision-making aspect of your job overwhelm you. If you are having trouble making a decision, it is probably for one of two reasons: one, you do not have all the facts, or two, you are too close to the situation to be objective. "What I do when I find myself having trouble with a decision," says William Morgan, "is to step away from it and let it sit for a while—if it's at all possible. Then I find that when I least expect it, when I'm driving or doing something else, I'll think about it and get an entirely different slant on the subject."

One final thought on decision making—you rarely have to make a major decision alone. Good managers, in fact, routinely seek input from staff members before making any major policy or operations change. In Japan, before managers make any decision, they are expected to gain a consensus from all the key people to be affected by the decision. This may be taking things too far, but decisions reached in this manner serve two important functions: one, they carry with them built-in acceptance; two, they take the burden of being right or wrong off the manager.

HOW TO TELL WHEN A STAFF MEMBER IS ABOUT TO QUIT

The last people you want on your staff are those who, for whatever reason, are looking elsewhere. The problem, though, is that most people looking for another job do their best to keep the news from their employers until they find something else. However, there are some signs that will give you an indication that somebody is planning to leave.

1. *Longer lunch hours:* Staff members who begin taking noticeably longer lunch hours could well be using the time for job interviews.

2. *Frequent absences:* Like longer lunch hours, a sudden increase in

absences might indicate that the person is taking time off to go on job interviews.

3. *An increase in personal phone calls:* The calls may be coming from potential employers setting up interviews.

4. *Any change in communication attitude:* Take notice when a normally aggressive employee begins to act docile at staff meetings or a normally docile employee begins to act aggressive. It could mean that the employee no longer cares what management thinks.

5. *A change in vacation pattern:* Some employees who are planning an intensive job interview period will request an immediate vacation.

6. *A neater desk:* If the desk of an employee who usually has a sloppy desk suddenly appears neater than usual, it could mean that the employee is beginning to clear out personal belongings.

7. *A sudden improvement in grooming or appearance:* When staff members show up for work noticeably better dressed and groomed, they could be dressed that way because of job interviews.

WHAT TO DO ABOUT AN EMPLOYEE WHO PLANS TO LEAVE

If you have reason to think that a staff member is about to leave, your best policy is to act immediately. You should speak to this person and ask pointedly, "Are you looking to change jobs?" Most people will not lie to you when you confront them directly.

If the employee is somebody you want to stay, make an effort to reconcile differences. In some cases, a long talk in which you discuss the employee's future will bring problems to light and perhaps iron some of them out. On the other hand, if the person tells you, "I've just accepted a job," resist the temptation to make a counteroffer. Counteroffers, when accepted, will encourage other employees to use the same tactic. In addition, studies have shown that an employee who accepts a counteroffer rarely stays more than a year.

WHEN FIRING BECOMES NECESSARY

Firing is something every good manager has to do now and then, and no manager ever gets accustomed to it. Probably the only consolation in the difficulty of firing someone is that surveys show most employees who get fired actually expect it, even though the day of reckoning may come as a shock.

Just as there is an art to hiring the right people, there is an art to terminating people. Here are a few principles to keep in mind:

1. *Do it in person:* If you hired the person who is to be fired, it is your responsibility to handle the firing and to do it in person. This is one responsibility you should never delegate.

2. *Do not drag it out:* Be tactful, but deliver the news early in the conversation. The longer you wait to give the bad news, the harder it is for the employee.

3. *Have all necessary information on hand:* The employee you let go has a right to know immediately whatever benefits are due. Have an adequate separation payment and the final check at the meeting.

4. *Be extra tactful:* Without lying, do your best to give the departing employee an explanation that he or she can live with. The last thing you want is a bitter ex-employee.

5. *Analyze what went wrong:* Our surveys indicate that most top executives place the blame on management when an employee is fired. You have to ask yourself what led you to hire the person in the first place and what you can do to prevent yourself from hiring the same type of person again.

RATE YOURSELF AS A MANAGER

The following test should give you a general idea of how well you manage (assuming that you have a managerial position). If you are not a manager as yet, you could take the test anyway and answer the questions according to how you think you *might* perform as a manager. To take the test, answer each question on a scale of 1 to 5, with 5 indicating that you almost always do what the question asks and 1 indicating that you never or hardly ever do it. When you have finished, you can rate yourself on a scale of 1 to 100.

1. When you need to hire a new staff member, do you take the time and make the effort necessary to hire the best possible person for the job? _____

2. Do you take the time to orient new staff members so that they understand not only their own jobs but also how their jobs fit into the overall scheme of things? _____

3. Are you aware of the strengths and weaknesses of each of your staff members? _____

4. Do you set the example you want your staff members to follow? _____

5. Do you show a sincere interest in your staff members as *people*, rather than simply as subordinates? _____

6. Are you aware of the career aspirations of each of your staff members? _____

7. Do you make it a point (if practicable) to meet one on one with individual members of your staff? _____

8. Are you careful not to show favoritism to any member or members of your staff? _____

9. Do all the members of your staff have clearly defined responsibilities and the authority to carry out these responsibilities? _____

10. Do you have enough confidence in your staff members to trust their decisions on matters relating to their responsibilities? _____

11. When appropriate, do you involve your staff members in important decisions? _____

12. Do you try your best at staff meetings to encourage objective observations from members of your staff? _____

13. When you make assignments, are you sensitive to the workload? _____

14. Do you set *reasonable* deadlines when you make assignments? _____

15. Do you vary your supervisory style according to the personality of the staff member? _____

16. Do you make it a point to praise your staff members (when praise is justified) on a regular basis? _____

17. When you criticize staff members, do you try your best to be constructive? _____

18. Do you concern yourself with the advancement rate of your better staff members and do you help them as best you can to get ahead? _____

19. When a staff member quits, do you conduct an exit interview in order to determine the reasons for leaving? _____

20. Do you take time every now and then to evaluate your managerial effectiveness? _____

Becoming a Better Communicator

7

The ability to communicate is the link between your knowledge and your success.

Recently, researchers at the University of Michigan Graduate School of Business asked a group of newly promoted executives to name the courses they considered most important for business success and the results of the survey added up to both good news and bad news for accountants. The good news is that finance and accounting came out very high in the survey, well ahead of courses having to do with production, marketing, and advertising. The bad news is that the course that came out number one in the survey was communication—written and oral.

The reason I describe this finding as "bad news" for accountants should be obvious by now. As I mentioned earlier, only about 6 per cent of the top management personnel we queried in our Burke study gave high marks to the communication skills of public accountants, and only 8 per cent of top management felt that the communication skills of management accountants were particularly strong. The survey also showed that 96 per cent of CPA partners and 94 per cent of chief financial officers felt it was easier for articulate accountants to get ahead in public accounting, and 100 per cent had the same thing to say about management accountants who are articulate.

Considering that we are talking here about the most basic of management skills, I find these figures enormously significant, particularly since it is generally agreed that the inability to communicate effectively is probably the number one reason why otherwise competent accountants have trouble moving up. "The accountants I've known who have difficulty moving up," says Michael Goldstein, "are almost always weak in communication skills. Yet, this is the one skill that is simply not taught in any accounting school." It goes without saying, too, that the ability to communicate well when you speak and write enhances your managerial ability and simply makes you more *efficient* at your job.

My friend Harold M. Messmer, Jr., President of Boothe Financial Corporation, commented to me, "In my career, I've hired many financially oriented employees, and came to the conclusion there are many variables that could add up to making them successful at their jobs." And then he added, "But, over the years, I've found that those accountants who do not communicate well are doomed to failure, or will most certainly never achieve their full potential."

Nor does the importance of your ability to communicate well diminish once you reach the top. Consider Hays Wilkins, an accountant who rose from staff management accountant to CEO of CSX, the company created by the merger of Chessie System, Inc. and Seaboard Coast Line Industries, Inc. "Communication," Wilkins says, "is the most important part of my job and most important part of any job." He goes on to emphasize that, while it helps your career to have great ideas, you are in trouble if you cannot communicate them. "Make it so simple," he advises, "that even the president of the company can understand it."

Wilkins is not suggesting company presidents lack the ability to *understand* information. Their problem, as he puts it, is having the time, circumstances, and luxury of taking the time to understand something. He concludes: "In this fast world, I have to learn the meanings of things rather quickly."

No need to belabor the point. Become a better communicator and it cannot help but enhance your chances for career success. What I would like to share with you throughout the rest of this chapter are some thoughts on communication that you can either use immediately or build upon in your own way.

DEVELOPING YOUR WRITING ABILITY

Nearly every job in accounting and all but a handful of middle to upper management jobs in business require you to communicate your thoughts in writing, whether it be in memos, reports, letters to clients, or, in some cases, articles in trade journals. Writing, in other words, is not merely a *skill* but a basic tool in the accounting profession, and whatever you can do to improve your ability to use this tool will almost invariably enhance your career progress.

There are any number of different ways you can develop your ability to write more effectively—from how-to books on writing to writing courses and seminars. But the key to becoming a more effective writer begins, in my view, with a basic decision that you *want* to improve this ability and that you will put in the time and effort necessary to promote this improvement.

I myself have never had a problem putting in the time and effort because I have always enjoyed writing. Yet, I am aware, based on my conversations with professional writers and with other business executives, that I am something of an exception and that for most people, even those who do it well, writing is difficult—even painful. "Regardless of how accomplished you are at the craft," notes Barry Tarshis, who is both a successful professional writer and a communications consultant,

> writing never becomes something you can do without effort and concentration. It's very much like a sport. You can be the most talented golfer in the world, but if you don't concentrate and apply yourself each time you go out to a golf course, you're never going to be very happy with your scores.

FIVE KEYS TO MORE EFFECTIVE WRITING

There are no "secrets" to effective writing in business. In the end, it is a matter of being in command of your information and being able to use skills you learned in high school and college to present this information clearly and concisely. But, while there are no secrets, there are several techniques and principles that I have found useful myself and that I think can help you. Here are five of the most important:

1. Adopt a more efficient writing routine: Writing is a skill and, as with any skill, your ability to execute it cannot help but be affected by the habits you follow and by the conditions in which you try to do it.

Put simply, you cannot take writing for granted. As any seasoned writing professional will tell you, writing demands concentration, and to try to write an important report or memo at the same time you are juggling four or five other tasks is tantmount to trying to play your best round of golf while you are thinking about how to operate your new computer.

So, effective writing principle number one is to try to create a routine and conditions conducive to writing. In particular, you need a place where you can concentrate (if your office is too hectic, consider doing your writing in a conference room). You also need to set aside blocks of time in which you can focus on your writing without being interrupted. The best way to assure yourself this time is to set aside specific time periods in your schedule devoted exclusively to whatever writing you need to accomplish that day.

How will you find the time? I cannot say. What I *can* say, though, is this: if you added up the amount of time most accountants who have no specific writing schedule spend on a typical writing chore, my guess is that this total would far exceed the amount of time it would take if they would simply set aside a certain amount of *uninterrupted* time.

As far as an actual writing "system" goes, it is best to thinking of writing, at the very least, as a two-stage process. In the first of the two stages, your concern should be the content and organization of your material, and not the actual style of the writing, on which you should focus only after the content and organization have been addressed. You can often get by with *combining* these two functions on very routine correspondence, but as soon as you begin writing something sensitive or complicated, combining the two stages almost invariably makes the process much more difficult. The reason: you are forcing your brain simultaneously to perform two functions that are not especially compatible: one, deciding *what* to say; and, two, deciding *how* to say it.

A better alternative is, once you have roughed out your thoughts in list or outline form, to see if you get a reasonably complete first draft on paper, without worrying that every word you choose is the word you will eventually want to use. Then, once this draft is on paper, go back and do the polishing and editing.

2. Be certain of your objective. You never write simply to *write* in business. The writing always has some business-related objective: it has to *accomplish* something. The purpose behind many of the routine documents you write as an accountant, of course, will be to communicate financial information, but it would be wrong to assume that communicating information is the *only* objective you need to think about when you are communicating financial information. More often than you might imagine, you need to produce an action with your writing: convince someone to *do* something (or not do something) or influence a management decision.

The distinction between the information you need to communicate and what that information is meant to accomplish may seem inconsequential, but it is a distinction you should never lose sight of. Otherwise, you will fall into the all-too-common trap of producing documents that read well enough but have little or no impact on the situation that led you to write in the first place. If you are writing to a client, for example, your objective—in addition to simply communicating—is to reinforce the relationship you have established with the client. If you are writing a memo to one of your staff members who has not been as detail-minded as you like, your ultimate purpose is not to express your dissatisfaction. It is to motivate your staff member to pay more attention to details.

With this difference in mind, the tone and the style of your writing become almost as important as the information you need to communicate, which means that the tone you strike in your writing will vary according to your objective. Just as in conversation, there is a time to be personal and accommodating and a time to be firm. You need to adjust your tone to the situation. First, though, you need to decide what you want to achieve.

3. Focus on thoughts, not numbers. The focus of the writing you do as an accountant will often be numbers, but the people reading what you write, more often than not, are mainly interested in the information that lies behind these numbers. This principle is particularly important if you are in management accounting and the people to whom you are writing are using your financial analyses to make decisions. Indeed, one of the complaints voiced most frequently by senior management when discussing the writing skills of management accountants is that it often takes them too much time and effort to discern *meaning* in numbers.

It is hard to say exactly how far you should go when interpreting the numbers you are presenting because it will vary according to your individual situation. As a general rule, though, the more you can position yourself when you write as not simply the conveyer of numbers but as an analyst and a problem-solver, the more valuable you are going to be to those who rely on you for financial information.

4. Get to the point early. Whatever you are writing, whether it is a memo or a letter, get into the habit of indicating as early in the document as possible why you are writing and what, in general, you are expecting of your reader. Occasionally, when you are dealing with a sensitive subject or have some bad news to deliver, you might want to deviate from this principle and write an introductory paragraph designed to make the reader a more receptive to the bad news. For the most part, though, you will help yourself immensely if you make sure that, by the time your readers are into the second paragraph of your document, they know at least two things: one, why you are writing; and, two, why they should care enough to read on.

5. Write in a simple, direct style. Some accountants seem to think that, the more obscure and jargonistic they are when they write, the more impressed their audience is likely to be. I do not agree. The most effective communicators I have known during my career—Malcolm Forbes, for instance—write in a simple, almost conversational style. They use words the way words were intended to be used: to express ideas clearly and concisely.

In certain types of financial writing, of course, you need to follow relatively strict stylistic guidelines. In audit reports, for instance, it is generally accepted that you express certain types of information in the so-called passive voice ("It was found that . . ."), rather than the more personal and direct active voice ("I found . . .). Moreover, there are certain financial terms that you have little choice but to use even though the general public might not be familiar with them.

On the other hand, when it comes to less formal forms of communication—personal letters or even business letters, for example—a highly formal, starchy sort of style becomes more difficult to justify, particularly with the emphasis today on plain language in financial documents.

What follows is a brief list of phrases that fall into the category of businessese and the plain words that express the same thought much more concisely. Use this list as a foundation to build your own.

Instead of:	This:
In the eventuality that	If
In the majority of instances	Usually
The manner in which	How
At what location	Where
For the reason that	Because
Based on the fact that	Because
In light of the fact that	Because
At what point in time	When
At the present time	Now
With regard to	About
At some time in the near future	Soon
Until such time that	Until
Achieve the objective we want to accomplish	Succeed
Within the realm of manageability	Manageable

PUBLIC SPEAKING

More and more these days, the ability to communicate your ideas orally to a group has become an essential skill for accountants, particularly as you move further into management. If you are like the majority of people, however, the thought of speaking in front of a group is enough to make your palms sweat. Surveys show, in fact, that many people fear public speaking more than death, flying, or loneliness.

With this observation in mind, I am not going to promise that what I have to say about speaking in this chapter will turn you into an accomplished speaker, but my suggestions should give you a good foundation; they have proven useful to me personally and to many people I know who have taught themselves to be effective speakers.

GAINING PERSPECTIVE

I once asked one of the best after dinner speakers I ever met what he considered to be the most important ingredient in becoming more effective in front of a group. "Three things," he said without missing a beat. "Practice. Practice. Practice."

Practice does indeed help. But more important than practice is actual experience. For the more you become accustomed to speaking in front of groups, the easier the experience will become for you. I doubt whether the experience will ever become *so* routine that you will not feel a trace of butterflies, but the more you speak in front of groups, the more you will come to realize that you do not have to be a spellbinder to be effective. You will recognize, for example, that your audience is mainly interested in the information you are sharing with them—they do not expect to be entertained. In other words, you do not have to be *that* good at public speaking in order to communicate your information effectively. What is important is that your presentation be well organized and that the information you give be relevant to your audience.

Another thing you will come to realize with experience is that unless you are *excessively* nervous—and most people are not—the audience is not likely even to notice your apprehension. I can remember on any number of occasions when I first began speaking how nervous I felt and how surprised I was afterward when people came to me and complimented me on how relaxed I seemed. One of the best speakers I know—a lawyer who is in constant demand at conventions—conquered his fear of speaking in front of a group by continually reminding himself that the butterflies in his stomach were invisible to the audience.

THE IMPORTANCE OF PREPARATION

Unless you have proved to yourself that you can get by without it, make absolutely certain that, by the time you find yourself in front of the group you are addressing, you are in absolute command of your information. This does not necessarily mean that you should have your speech or presentation memorized. It means simply that you should feel comfortable not only with the information you are delivering but with any visual aids—charts, for instance—you intend to use.

There are any number of ways you can prepare for your talk. At the very least, however, you should have the basic information under control at least three or four weeks before you are scheduled to speak. You should be aware of the following:

How long the speech or presentation is likely to take

How large the audience is likely to be and who, exactly, will be in that audience

Whether there will be a question and answer period

Whether you will be using a podium, microphone, etc.

The object of all this preparation is very simple: you want to avoid last-minute surprises. Recently, I heard about an editor who was invited to give a talk before a group of corporate communication specialists but, for some reason, never bothered to find out any particulars. The editor arrived with a prepared 40-minute speech only to discover that, for one thing, she was expected to speak for only 15 minutes, and, in addition, the people in her group did not hold the jobs she thought they would, which meant that her talk had almost no relevance. She survived the experience—barely.

If possible, try ahead of time to visit the room in which you will be giving the talk. If it is an auditorium, walk on the stage and see if you can get a sense of how it feels to be in front of the podium. Professional athletes go through this exercise all the time. Shortly after she won the Wimbledon championships several years ago, the English tennis star Virginia Wade revealed that, on the morning of the finals, she walked out on Centre Court, empty as it was, and went through the mental exercise of seeing herself walking on the court later that day, with the stands filled to capacity. Wade insists that her visualization helped to reduce the attack of nerves that usually struck whenever she was about to play a big match.

LOOKING YOUR BEST

Even before you speak, your audience will be making judgments about you, based on your appearance. For this reason alone (apart from the way you feel about yourself), you always want to look your best when you are making any sort of presentation. In most cases, you will want to choose clothing that conveys a strong sense of profession-alism, but it is also important that you feel *comfortable* in whatever you are wearing. Think twice, for instance, before deciding to break in a new pair of shoes on the day you are set to give a presentation.

GIVING THE TALK

How effective you are when the time comes to actually deliver the speech will depend on a variety of factors, but here are the elements of speaking in front of a group that, according to experts, account for the biggest differences between effective and ineffective speakers.

Your posture: The general rule is to stand erect—but not too stiff—with your feet solidly planted about a shoulder's width apart. If there is a podium, it is all right to lean forward occasionally, and if you have a portable microphone (or are not using a microphone), there is nothing wrong with moving around the stage or dais. Be careful, though. If you move around too much, your movements can detract from your talk. And, make sure that you do not get into the habit of swaying back and forth. That, too, like any mannered gesture, can interfere with your talk.

Your voice: The best advice I can give about using your voice effectively when you speak in front of a group is to be as natural as you can and not make the mistake of trying to sound like somebody you are not. Keep in mind that you do not have to sound like a TV anchor person to hold an audience. Consider Art Buchwald, who is an extremely successful speaker even though his voice is thin and nasal.

More important than the individual quality of your voice is how you use it. Most novice speakers make the same two mistakes. First, they do not speak loud enough. Second, they speak too fast. So, if you do nothing more than slow down your delivery and force yourself to speak louder than you normally would, you will be that far ahead of the game.

How you vary your tone is important, too. Accomplished speakers are able to raise and lower their voices at strategic points in the presentation. They will use muted tones when they want to make a serious point and will raise their voices when they want to generate enthusiasm. In any event, the "right" voice is the one matches your purpose.

One of the best ways to learn how to use pace and tone more effectively is to make the speech into a tape recorder and then play it back. When you practice, vary the volume, pitch, and tone of your voice. This will give you an idea of the effect you are able to achieve when you vary your voice. Be careful, too, of those common phrases ("You know," "Like I say," "In the final analysis"), and also of distracting words ("um," "uh," and "well").

Establish eye contact: Good eye contact is essential for establishing rapport with your audience. Once again, the watchword is *natural.* Look at the entire group, but avoid darting glances. Look at specific individuals in the group for several seconds at a time, making an effort to speak personally on a one-to-one level with each person. This will help you conquer nervousness and alleviate any self-conscious feelings. It is also an excellent way for you to "read" the audience. If you see people yawning or looking at the clock, this usually signals audience boredom. On the other hand, smiles and nods can be a very reassuring indication that you and your speech are interesting.

Gestures: The right gesture at the right time can add vitality to a speech, but, here again, the key is to be natural and not to force. When posing a thoughtful question, touching your finger gently to your temple can be memorable. When asking for a show of hands on a debatable point, raising yours will be seen as a perfectly natural gesture.

ELICITING QUESTIONS FROM YOUR AUDIENCE

Except on very formal occasions, it is usually a good idea to leave some time after your speech for members of the audience to ask questions. The only danger here is that your invitation for questions may produce an awkward silence and end the speech on a down note.

There are three ways to prevent this from happening. The first is to insist that the program chairperson arrange to distribute forms to the audience so that they can write down questions. When you are a little more than half-way through with your speech the chairperson will arrange for assistants unobtrusively to pick up the questions and deliver them to the chairperson, who will identify the best ones to ask you at the end of your prepared talk. This method is necessary when your audience is larger than 150 people. For smaller groups, the second method of being assured of getting questions started is to arrange ahead of time for a friend or colleague to ask the first question (usually, when one question has been asked, others quickly follow). The third option is to start the ball rolling yourself with a statement such as, "One of the questions I'm frequently asked is. . . ."

Once questions start coming in, here are some pointers on how to keep things moving without surrendering control.

1. Repeat the question you have been asked so that everybody in the audience knows what you are answering

2. Make sure you understand the question before you start answering it, and do not be embarrassed, if you are not sure of the question's meaning, to ask the person to repeat it

3. Break complex questions down into simpler parts (it's a good idea, if you do this, to check with the person who asked the question to make sure you have not misrepresented the question)

4. Keep your answers as brief as possible, but always refer back to the questioner to make sure you have answered the question to his or her satisfaction

5. Do not be afraid to admit you do not know—as embarrassing as it might be to plead ignorance, it will be twice as embarrassing to get be in a lie (*the best approach:* admit that you do not have the answer at your fingertips but say that you would be happy to find out more for the person)

6. Watch your tone—not every question you are asked will be a question you consider worth answering, but try not to indicate your displeasure or impatience with a curt reply

You may occasionally run into some hostile questions during a question and answer period, and it pays to know how to deal with these situations.

The most important thing is to stay in control, regardless of how hostile the questioner may be. You should give the person attacking you a chance to speak his or her piece, but if the person is, in effect, taking the platform away from you, there is nothing wrong with interrupting (politely but firmly) and suggesting that the two of you discuss the problem later. It is a mistake to *ignore* the hostile question (doing so will hurt your credibility). A better strategy would be to grant to the person taking issue with you that he or she certainly has the right to disagree, but that you do not happen to go along with that position. Above all, do not be lured into a battle of name-calling. Keep your cool. Maintain your dignity. And let pressure from the audience put people who are extremely rude in their place.

PRIVATE SPEAKING

Almost everything I have said about public speaking applies to business and social meetings, and to ordinary conversations with colleagues or friends. The main thing to remember in "private speaking" is that you do not own the floor, and you must be prepared to make your point and let someone else voice an opinion. Sharing the floor is extremely important. The consequence of not sharing is that almost everything you say after a certain amount of time is heard but not assimilated because the other parties are too busy organizing their thoughts to pay much attention to you.

What should you do if someone else is hogging the floor, and you, and others, have difficulty getting a word in edgewise? Here is what I do. When the hog pauses to breathe, I quickly make a statement to or ask a question of the person farthest away from the constant talker. This invariably ends the filibuster.

How to Market Yourself

8

Selling yourself is the most important and most difficult sale you can make.

Not very long ago—as recently as 1978—a chapter on marketing yourself would have been out of place in a book directed to accountants. Prior to the 1978 change in the Code of Professional Conduct that removed the prohibition against advertising and public relations programs for CPAs, most accountants thought little about marketing. It was considered unethical, for instance, for public accountants actively to solicit clients who were being serviced by another accountant. And, while it was all right to "develop a practice," it was not considered appropriate to take direct steps to promote your name; you had to be low-keyed and subtle.

Today, attitudes are changing. The idea that you never go directly to potential clients and ask them for business is, as far as many firms are concerned, a thing of the past. More and more firms are not only advertising their services but also hiring professionals to handle their public relations.

Even given these changes in the profession as a whole, a great many accountants are still uncomfortable with the idea of marketing their companies and promoting themselves. A survey by the AICPA a few years ago revealed that two-thirds of its members still had negative attitudes toward uninvited solicitation and were still uncomfortable with the idea of seeking publicity, and there is no reason to think that management accountants are any less skittish about promoting themselves.

It is obvious, too, that most accountants do not do nearly enough to promote *themselves.* "A lot of accountants do a very adequate technical job," says Philip Chenok,

> but do not get recognized. They are not known, they don't promote themselves in the company or outside the company. They don't write for the *Journal of Accountancy* or for state CPA society magazines or any professional publications. If they join a state CPA society, they don't show up at meetings and they don't attempt to get on committees. They go home, watch television, play with the kids, and go back to work the next day. I'm not saying you need to give up your social life, but I think to get ahead you need some visibility.

Why should accountants be this way? One possible reason is that many accountants simply do not know how to go about gaining visibility. A second reason may lie in the fact that many accountants are afraid of visibility. "With many accountants," says Isaac Assael, "it's a fear of putting themselves on the line. Some people are afraid that if they become well known, they'll become a target of criticism, and this may be why the general public has so little idea of what accountants do."

Whatever the reason why so many accountants are not very good at marketing themselves, the fact remains that the ability to market yourself can have as much bearing on your career progress as anything else you do.

GAINING RECOGNITION

It is a safe assumption that the more people who are aware of who you are and what you can do, the more likely it is that your career will keep advancing. How do you go about gaining recognition while you are struggling each day simply to keep up with your responsibilities?

There is no one answer to the question, and a lot will depend on your specialty. Management accountants and accountants working for CPA firms, for instance, are not in a position to promote themselves as actively as accountants who work for themselves. But, regardless of who you work for or what your specialty is, there are more ways than you might be aware of to gain recognition without devoting most of your time to the task and without violating any of the ethics of the accounting profession. Let us look at some of these ways.

GETTING INVOLVED IN ORGANIZATIONS

One of the easiest and most direct ways of gaining visibility is to become active in professional and community organizations. Indeed, if there is one thing in which nearly everyone at the top of the accounting profession believes, it is that the right kind of organizational involvement translates directly into career progress. Philip Chenok, for instance, recalls one managing partner of a medium-sized firm telling him about the time he devoted to the Institute (AICPA). Because he enjoyed the involvement so much, he ended up spending almost as much time working for the Institute as he did on his practice. "And the strange thing," says Chenok, "is that the more time this accountant devoted to the Institute, the more his practice grew and prospered."

There are any number of organizations the right kind of involvement in which can help your career. Joining professional associations, such as the American Institute of Certified Public Accountants, the National Association of Accountants, or your state CPA society, is essential, but it is not enough to join. To get the most out of these affiliations, you need to be active in them. You have to join and become active on committees (particularly those committees that relate to your specialty).

"The more you get involved," says Marshall Fudge, a chartered accountant who owns our Toronto office, "the more recognition you get from peers." Fudge himself is the example that proves the point. Beyond simply getting involved in professional organizations, he helped on professional development committees, marked examinations, and wrote articles. These kinds of activities, he maintains, help you whether you go into public or private accounting.

Your group involvements need not be limited to accounting. Dan Kramer, as I mentioned earlier, attributed the large number of entertainment clients that he had during his public accounting career to the fact that he was always very interested in classical music. Other accountants have parlayed their interest in sports or civic organizations into more visibility and greater career success. Apart from these kinds of groups, you might want to consider organizations like the local chamber of commerce (especially if you have a private practice). If you are a management accountant you should belong to the trade associations that relate to your industry.

We have only scratched the surface. In every community there are civic organizations, executive groups, religious groups, educational groups, alumni associations, and country clubs. Clearly, you do not have the time to join all of them, so be selective. You are better off,

I believe, being *active* and visible in a few organizations than being a name on countless membership rosters. To repeat, try to get active on those committees that deal with your field of interest. If you are a tax accountant, you should be on the tax committee and, ideally, should be heading it. Being the head says to the outside world that you are an expert. (Don't you tend to assume that the chief of surgery at a hospital is the best surgeon?)

Political parties, too, represent good opportunities for useful affiliations, albeit with some qualifications. Make sure, for one thing, that the job you do for the party relates in some way to your career interest. Also, do not allow your partisan politics to spill over into your office or, if you are a practicing CPA, to your clients. As long as you are careful about these things, most firms will not mind your getting involved in politics. Many, in fact, encourage these involvements.

All in all, then, the thing to remember about organizations is to choose the ones you become active in with care. Concentrate mainly on groups and affiliations in which you are likely to make the most contacts and your involvement will do the most to enhance your reputation.

GETTING INTO PRINT

Few things you do as an accountant will help your career more than getting articles published in trade and business journals. "If you can write well," notes Dr. Emanuel Saxe, "you have a built-in means of advertising yourself." Getting articles published makes you more of an authority. It looks good to your current company and it gets other firms interested in you. I can tell you from firsthand experience that personnel directors as well as recruiters follow articles in trade journals closely.

Writing articles can be especially difficult if, like most accountants, you have never done much writing. On the other hand, there is no great mystery to writing. I have never taken a writing course in my life, but I write well enough to get published, because I have worked hard on my writing. More important, I enjoy it and set aside time for it.

If you lack confidence in your ability to write, as I emphasized in the last chapter, consider this: it is your expertise and your ideas that publications are looking for, and not your writing skills. As long as the article is reasonably well organized and the information is accurate and pertinent, the editors will do the final editing.

COMING UP WITH ARTICLE IDEAS

One of the best things about being an accountant is that you have expertise in a subject that almost everybody is interested in: money. Coming up with ideas of interest to editors, in other words, should not be much of a problem—assuming you are willing to focus on this aspect of your career in a reasonably organized fashion.

To begin with, you should keep a file of possible article ideas; use that file to store clippings on subjects that might lend themselves to articles. Particularly good sources are subjects that are being covered widely in the news. I know of a CPA in business for herself who increased her practice by nearly 20 per cent through a series of articles she wrote on tax reform for her local community newspaper. The articles were short—no more than 300 words—and each one dealt with a specific aspect of the new law, such as charitable donations or real estate. There was nothing spectacular about the articles: each consisted of a short lead that introduced the topic, three or four specific points presented bullet-style, and a wrap-up paragraph that offered general advice on how to plan one's own finances in light of the new law. Except for the short biography line at the end of the article, there was no blatant pitch for business in any of the articles, but the articles did a lot to position the accountant as an expert. By writing a *series* of short articles, she was able to keep her name in print for four consecutive weeks.

I cannot emphasize enough how eager most editors of local community newspapers are to publish articles by professionals who have expertise in subjects that their readers are interested in. At issue, then, is not whether you can get such articles published. You certainly *can.* At issue is whether you are willing to take the time to gather the information and write such articles—or, to put it another way, whether the benefits of having by-lined articles justify the time you spend.

SAMPLE QUERY LETTER

July 10, 1987

Susan Evans
Editor
State Business Digest
14 Monroe St.
Chicago, IL 60601

Dear Ms. Evans:

The new tax law, as you undoubtedly know, has eliminated many of the deductions for interest and has created the impression that home equity loans are an excellent way to reduce taxes. What many people do not realize, however, is that the new tax law sets limits on how much mortgage interest is deductible, which means that such loans might not make good sense for many of the people who are now applying for them.

As a CPA and financial advisor, I have been counseling many of my clients on this very issue, and I would like to propose a brief article on this subject for your Personal Finance column. The article I'm suggesting would present a clear picture of how the new tax law is affecting mortgage interest deductions and would set down some guidelines that would allow readers to decide for themselves if an equity loan makes sense.

If you would like to discuss this subject further, I would be happy to do so. I could also have this article on your desk within a few days after you give me the go-ahead.

Enclosed you will find a copy of an article I recently published in our state accounting journal. It is naturally a little more technical than the article I'm proposing would be, but it should give you a general idea of how I write.

Looking forward to hearing from you.

Sincerely,

George Patterson

GETTING ARTICLES PUBLISHED

I have known accountants who, without being asked, have sent in finished articles to publications and had them published, but I do not recommend this strategy. Under most circumstances, unsolicited articles do *not* get published (some magazines will not even accept them). In other words, you could be wasting a lot of effort.

The recommended procedure is to write a letter to the editor of the publication in which you briefly outline the kind of article you would like to write. Professional writers call this a query letter, and here, from *How to Write Like a Pro*, by Barry Tarshis, are the guidelines to follow:

1. Be brief.

2. Make sure that the idea you suggest (*a*) is appropriate for the magazine you're writing to and (*b*) has not been covered by that magazine recently.

3. If you can make some personal connection early in the letter ("Jane Doe suggested I write you. . . ."), do so.

4. Be upbeat and positive, but don't oversell your idea. Avoid overstatements and don't hit the editor over the head with how much the article is needed. Let the editor decide.

5. Be as specific as you can in outlining the general content of the article.

6. Try to write naturally. When in doubt, write the same as you speak.

Should you get the go-ahead to do the article, you'll be given a deadline, and I would urge you, particularly if this is your first article, to meet that deadline. If you are going to be late with the article, notify the publication well in advance. Apart from looking for accountants who know how to write, editors are anxious for accountants who can meet deadlines. The easier you make life for them, the more likely they will be to invite you to write more articles.

WRITING LETTERS TO THE EDITOR

One of the simplest ways of getting your name known is to write letters to the editor. Do not waste your time writing about issues that do not relate to your specialty—unless you can demonstrate something in the letter about your broad financial and business expertise. Regardless of how you might feel, say, about the dog-leash law or a new parking regulation in your town, a letter on these topics will not enhance your reputation as much as a letter that promotes the idea that you are an authority and a specialist. Also, the impression your letter makes on the reader should enhance your reputation as an authority.

There are some purely technical ground rules to follow when writing a letter to an editor. Your letter should be about the same length as other letters the publication prints. (Unless your name is Henry Kissinger, few newspapers or magazines will publish a letter that will fill most of the Letters to the Editor section.)

Another thing you have to be careful about when you write a letter to the editor is keeping the tone calm and factual. Apart from the fact that anger and emotion are difficult to convey effectively in a letter, editors usually worry about anything too incendiary. Finally, keep the focus of the letter as narrow as possible. Pick one topic, issue, or idea and try to stick to it throughout the letter.

The letter in Exhibit 2, which was published in the *Wall Street Journal*, illustrates the points I've just made. I wrote it in response to an article by Frank R. Beaudine. In his article, Beaudine made the point that some search consultants are troubled by candidates who insist that they be called only at home because "it conveys a feeling of insecurity."

I disagree. Far from showing insecurity, a person who has the recruiter call at home is prudent. Note that in the letter I get to the point immediately. Note, too, that even though I disagree with Beaudine's views, I do not attack him personally, and I am careful about my tone. I also kept the letter brief. One other thing: I sent the letter by Federal Express, which means that the paper got it the next day, and it undoubtedly stood out on the editor's desk.

LETTERS TO THE EDITOR
Call Me at Home

Frank R. Beaudine, "Manager's Journal—What to Do When the Executive Recruiter Calls" (Dec. 27), writes: "Note of caution: Some search consultants are troubled by candidates who insist that they can be called only at home. It conveys the feeling of insecurity.

In my judgment candidates at all levels have to be concerned about jeopardizing their positions—particularly in these economic times. It is awkward, inappropriate and dangerous to conduct employment interviews on their employers' time. Candidates who request that recruiting calls be made to their homes are both sensible and prudent.

In addition, candidates who defer calls until after hours are showing respect for their current employers. People have every right to change jobs, but they should do it with maximum consideration for their employers and minimum risk to themselves.

Robert Half
Chairman
Robert Half International Inc.

EXHIBIT 2. Letter to the Editor. [Reprinted from *The Wall Street Journal*. December 30, 1982, with permission.]

PUBLIC SPEAKING

Like the ability to write well enough for publication, the ability to speak in front of groups can greatly enhance your image and increase your visibility. And, as I pointed out in the last chapter, the only thing holding most accountants back in this area is lack of confidence.

An excellent way to gain more confidence as a public speaker is to begin speaking in front of groups that will give you the opportunity to gain experience but carry no risk to your reputation. For instance, the guidance counselor at your local high school would probably welcome the idea of your talking to a senior class about career opportunities in accounting. A local retiree club would undoubtedly be interested in what you might have to tell them about financial management. Once you have gained a little confidence, you can branch out to some of the local social, civic, and religious groups, all of which look regularly for knowledgeable speakers.

To make things easy for yourself, you should develop two or three 20-minute to 30-minute speeches on general subjects that you can talk about in front of most groups. Here are some suggestions:

What to do when the IRS calls

Fringe benefit programs for employees

How to manage household expenses

How to start your own business

Setting up your own accounting system

As far as preparing the speech goes, you have a couple of options. One is to hire a free-lance writer to write the speech for you. The other is to do it yourself, which is not as difficult as you may think. Just make sure you keep your sentences short and your tone conversational. Remember, you are giving a speech, not a technical paper, and whatever you do, don't *read* the speech from a prepared text. Speak from brief notes. One page, 8½″ × 11″, should suffice for a half-hour talk.

Your opening is particularly important, but a good opening, contrary to what many people think, does not have to include a joke. In fact, unless you are an accomplished storyteller and are sure of a laugh, you should not try to be funny at the start of a speech. If the joke does not work, it makes everybody feel ill at ease.

The best openings are anecdotes—provided, that is, that they relate to the theme of your speech. If you want to give the anecdote more credibility, make yourself a part of it. Barring the anecdote, try a quote.

PUBLICIZING THE SPEECH

Usually, if you are giving a speech to an organization, its public relations manager will send press releases to local papers. (You'll need an up-to-date—and good—photograph of yourself, as well as a brief written biography.) In the event that the group has no such person, you must take it upon yourself to write the release and send it to the newspaper.

The release does not have to be elaborate. Here is how one might read:

> Local CPA to Speak
> at Friends of Library
> Meeting
> Linda Smith, a Certified Public Accountant with the firm of Jones and Smith, will be the featured speaker Monday evening, June 23, at the monthly Friends of Library meeting. Her topic will be *How to Start a Small Business*. Ms. Smith, a resident of Oakview for the pa seven years, is a graduate of State College. She spent four years with the CPA firm of Brown and Brown before joining with Alvin Jones last year. She has lectured on the topic of starting a small business for several local groups, including the Chamber of Commerce.
> Anyone interested in attending the talk should contact the Library.

The release should be sent to the attention of the business-financial editor. Make sure you include a good black-and-white glossy of yourself, at least 5" × 7". You could write a similar release *after* you have given the speech, in which case you would include a paragraph or two that summarizes the points covered in the talk.

TEACHING A COURSE

Another good way for accountants to become better known in their communities is through teaching. Granted, there are some drawbacks. Teaching, particularly part-time, does not pay much. It takes time. (In addition to classroom lectures, there are lessons to prepare and papers to mark.) Also, teaching could add yet another burden to what is already a busy schedule.

On the other hand, teaching—as long as it does not interfere with everything else you are trying to do—can be rewarding in more ways than one. Teaching builds your credibility as an authority. Teaching forces you to keep current and thus imposes a discipline that might not be there if you were not teaching. It also encourages you to improve your communications skills and in this way helps your self-confidence. Once you learn how to keep the attention of a class for an hour or two, a half-hour speech in front of a large group is not difficult at all.

If you are going to teach, keep a couple of things in mind. First of all, I would never take on more than one course per semester (particularly if I had never taught before) and, if possible, I would only teach a course that met for one night a week. I would also be sure to teach a subject I knew backward and forward.

The best source for a teaching job, and the source with which you will have the least trouble, is adult education classes through your high school. (They are a good place to gain experience.) Simply contact the school and let it know you're interested in teaching. Mention the subject you want to teach, the time you have available, and your credentials.

GETTING YOUR NAME IN PRINT

Entertainment celebrities spend thousands of dollars a year on publicists whose chief job is to get the celebrities' names mentioned in a newspaper or on television. You can do it a lot less expensively. For example, do your best to get to know local business writers. The reason—when business writers are researching articles, they often need authoritative quotes. Almost invariably, they seek out the people they know.

There are several ways you might get to know your local business writers better. One way is to ask among your friends whether anyone knows any of the business writers or editors and radio and TV personalities in your community and could introduce you to them. Another way is to attend special events—conferences, for instance—at which reporters are likely to be in attendance. Whenever you meet somebody connected with the media, introduce yourself and try to strike up a brief conversation. Follow up your discussion with a letter and perhaps an idea for an article.

Should a business writer eventually contact you to answer a question or make a comment, you should, of course, be as honest and forthright as possible. At the same time, be careful not to say anything that is going to get you in hot water with your firm or your clients. The best way to handle a sensitive question is to come right out and tell the reporter that you are not in a position to answer it. Unless you know the reporter very well—and even then you should be careful—do not give "off the record" comments. Most reporters will protect your identity, but you never know what kind of pressure the reporter is under to come up with a quote or a comment.

It is also a good idea, even though it takes a little time and effort, to act as an informal "stringer" for professional reporters. If you attend a state conference, for instance, send a copy of the proceedings along to the reporter, with a brief note that says something along the lines of, "thought you'd be interested in this." *Any* sort of article or clipping that you think would be of interest to reporters—whether it relates to you or not—is worth sending along from time to time. Even though the reporter may not use the information, the gesture will be appreciated. And, when the time comes for the reporter to quote an accountant, your name is likely to be foremost in that reporter's mind.

RADIO AND TELEVISION APPEARANCES

If the notion of appearing on a radio or television interview show seems outlandish to you, you could be selling yourself short. True, the possibilities of guest shots on shows like *Today* or *Good Morning America* are remote, but in your community there are any number of radio stations and, now, with cable spreading throughout the country, any number of television stations for which someone who can talk intelligently about finance would be in demand.

Your chances of being asked to appear on these shows will be greater, of course, if you have built up some sort of reputation through articles or through public speaking. But, even without this sort of reputation, there is nothing wrong with a brief letter to the producer of the show in which you describe how much you like the show and let your availability be known in the event that the show needs a financial specialist.

Should you be asked to appear on either a radio or a television program, enjoy the ego thrill for a few minutes and then get to work. Find out what sort of a show it is, who is doing the interviewing and who else (if anybody) is going to be on a panel. In most cases, you will be told ahead of time what the interviewer will ask you; in any case, you should decide in advance the key points you want to convey.

If it is your first media appearance, you can expect to be nervous, but there are a number of things you can do to keep your nervousness under control. I recommend, for instance, that you practice answering questions in front of a mirror or into a tape recorder. I am not talking about *memorizing* questions, but, by answering aloud some of the questions you are likely to be asked, you can frequently isolate points where you might stumble during the actual interview.

During the interview itself, the best advice is to relax—which, of course, is no advice at all. What *will* help in the interview, however, is to watch the person (not the camera) asking you the question and to *listen* carefully to the question. The idea here is to get your mind to focus on the conversation and not on the fact that you are on television. It is not a panacea, but it might work for you.

THE ULTIMATE MARKETING TOOL

Throughout this chapter I have been talking about some of the things you can do to market yourself better as an accountant, but I recognize that not all of these suggestions are applicable to everyone. There is, however, one principle of marketing that I consider all but universal in its application. I am talking here about your willingness to share your expertise, without always being paid for it.

Not every accountant (nor every lawyer) would agree with me on this point. I have known lawyers, for instance, who feel no compunction about sending a bill for information given during a five-minute phone conversation. Their thinking, in brief, is that the information they have is, in fact, the "product" they sell, and they are entitled to be paid.

I do not quarrel with the principle here, but there is a point at which carrying this principle too far can limit your success. It has always struck me as significant that the most successful professional people I know, particularly accountants and lawyers, are not at all hesitant to contribute their expertise during informal conversations. One lawyer in particular says he looks forward to those situations—at social events and even at his golf club—when people ask for his advice. He does not believe that he is *giving* this advice away. He sees it instead as a form of advertising. And, he insists that the clients he has gained by this generosity far outweigh whatever money he may have "lost" by giving out free advice.

This principle, by the way, applies not only to accountants in practice for themselves. It works as well in the corporate setting. Yes, you will always run into people who will try to take advantage of your knowledge, but, on balance, the more opportunities you take to position yourself as an authority, the greater the payoff in the long run.

How to Make the Right Job Move

9

There are few things in life
more important than your
career.

I do not care how good an accountant you are, what your present position is, or how satisfied you may be in your current position. Based on turnover statistics, there is a good chance that within a few years you are going to find yourself looking for another job. You are not likely to be fired, but maybe you will become bored with your present job. Maybe your firm will be involved in a merger that will leave you with less responsibility and a less promising career horizon. Or, maybe your firm will run into problems or bring in somebody above you with whom you have trouble getting along.

I am not trying to alarm you, but a basic principle of career planning is to be prepared for the unexpected. I have seen too many good accountants who, when suddenly faced with the prospect of finding a new job (for whatever reason), have made critical mistakes. They have taken jobs they should not have taken—jobs that not only diverted these accountants from their long-term career plans, but also often put them into dead-end situations. On the other hand, I have seen accountants whose careers have blossomed once they were forced to leave what they had thought was a secure position. In finding a new job, they also moved off in a career direction for which they were better suited.

In this chapter, we are going to focus on what you should—and should not—be doing when you find yourself looking for a new job. The point I am going to be stressing, above all, is that looking for a job is a job unto itself, and to be successful at this job—that is, to find the job that is right for you—you have to be as organized, as energetic, as diligent, and as hardworking as you would be in any job you have ever had.

WHEN TO THINK ABOUT LEAVING

There are two obvious reasons for leaving a job. The first is when you have no choice in the matter—you have been terminated or your firm seems to be doing its best to make life miserable for you. The second is when you have been offered a position that *clearly* is going to take you closer to your long-term career goal.

So much for the obvious situations. There are two less obvious times when it probably makes sense to leave a job. One is once you have begun to sense that your job is in jeopardy and prudence dictates that you jump before you are pushed. The other is when you have reached a decision that you have advanced about as far as you're going to advance in your present job and that if you do not make a move, your career will be stifled. Let us look at both situations.

HOW TO TELL WHEN YOUR JOB IS IN JEOPARDY

Except in the rarest of instances, you can sense ahead of time if your company may be preparing to let you go. Here are some of the key signs to look for:

1. *Consultants:* The sudden appearance of consultants often means that heads are going to roll. Often the consultants' findings reflect the preconceived opinions of management. If consultants are being brought in, find out who in management is bringing them in, and try to analyze whether or not you are in favor with them.

2. *Mergers:* Regardless of comments from old and new management that "no one will be replaced," mergers and acquisitions could mean trouble for you, depending on how the merger has been structured and how you are positioned in your company. In most cases, it is the people who work for the smaller firm and the firm that was acquired whose jobs are in the most jeopardy, particularly if there is a duplication of jobs.

3. *Silent treatment:* Even though they may not do it consciously,

bosses who are about to fire someone will make it a point to avoid that person.

4. *Lack of special assignments:* Not getting special assignments you have been accustomed to get is one of the most reliable signs that your job is in jeopardy. Accountants who are about to be fired are almost never asked to do special work prior to termination and obviously are not alerted to future assignments.

5. *No criticism:* When bosses who have made it a practice to criticize you suddenly stop the criticism, it may well mean that they have made up their minds that such criticism is a waste of time.

6. *Being left behind:* When those around you and below you are moving up and you are standing still, you can pretty much assume that you do not figure in your firm's long-range plans.

7. *Less responsibility:* When functions you have been handling routinely are transferred to someone else, do not be misled into thinking that the firm believes you have been working too hard. It may be a sign that they are thinking of replacing you but are waiting until they can locate and train the replacement.

8. *Business slump:* When business starts going bad, nobody's job is guaranteed. Your move, in the event business is bad and does not look as if it is going to get better, is to analyze how critical your job is to the operation. Be particularly concerned if you are a relative newcomer.

OTHER REASONS FOR LOOKING ELSEWHERE

Even when your job is *not* in jeopardy, there are still some situations in which your long-term career interests will be better served by looking elsewhere. Here are the key situations:

1. *You are dead-ended:* Most of the time, if you are honest with yourself, you can gauge your career prospects with your current firm. The simplest way to do this is to look at the positions above you, think about the people who are holding these positions, and ask yourself if someone with your background, credentials, and personal qualities would make a likely candidate.

2. *Your firm is not moving forward:* If your firm is not getting ahead, you are not likely to get ahead either. The question, though,

is why is the firm not doing better? Is it progressive enough? Has top management lost its touch with the marketplace? Has the firm's specialty lost its luster?

Let me stress here that unless the situation in your current job is intolerable, do not be too hasty about making a change. "If you're going to make a change," cautions Harry Gilbert, "make sure it's for the right reasons. Too often the job change is motivated by short-term impatience rather than a result of long-term career planning." Gilbert warns, in particular, about the "grass is always greener" syndrome in accounting. "A lot of accountants know somebody who has maximized job changes into major success stories," he says, "but what isn't recognized is the fact that in most success stories, the key was timing. The job changes were made only when the individuals were absolutely sure they could not do better where they already were."

There is no need to belabor the point. You are the only person who can determine whether your best interests will be served by staying in your current position or by looking elsewhere. But Harry Gilbert's advice seems to me to be well worth heeding. Says Gilbert: "If you're going to make a move, do it on the basis of *your* timing and *your* career goals, and not the fact that there may be just another job out there for you."

JOB HUNTING: SOME BASIC CONSIDERATIONS

In the event that you have decided (or it has been decided for you) to look for a new job, the most important thing to bear in mind is that looking for a job may be the hardest job you will ever have. To be successful—to get the kind of accounting job you truly want—you need to be energetic, persistent, and opportunistic. You cannot sit and wait for the job to find you. You have to find the job and then engineer a campaign to capture it. Above all, you must never forget that being qualified for a job is not enough to guarantee you that job. It is not necessarily the most qualified person who is hired; it is the person who is able to convince the person doing the hiring that he or she is the best person for the job.

Your approach to finding a job should be well organized. Whether you are working or not, you must still set aside a certain part of the week for your job search campaign. Many accountants have the mistaken belief that looking for jobs is mainly a matter of answering a few ads, sending out a few letters, and then sitting back and waiting for job interviews to materialize.

It does not work like that. Job hunting involves an enormous amount of digging, calling, and planning. If you are not working, you could be spending as many as 25 hours a week on your job hunt and still not have enough time to do what should be done. If you are working, the very least you should be willing to spend on your job campaign is 10 hours a week.

What should you be doing all this time? You should be scanning want ads, writing letters, talking to other accountants, researching companies that might interview you, and, probably most important, talking to people you know in order to find job leads. All of this is part of an organized job search routine. The tighter the system you devise to handle these tasks, the more successful your search is likely to be.

Apart from being well organized, there are a number of basic considerations in looking for a job that bear mention here. Some of them apply when you are out of work and looking. Others apply when you are still working. All of them are important.

1. *Keep up your appearance:* Looking for a job (whether you are working or not) can be a stressful situation and, if you are not careful, your appearance will suffer. As important as appearance is to your career success when you're working, it is doubly important when you are looking for work. Make sure whatever clothes you wear to interviews bring out the best in you. If necessary, buy *new* clothes. I know of some employment counselors who advise their clients to take a vacation before launching a job search. My advice is not to waste the time. Take the money you would have spent on a vacation and buy some clothes that will make you look good and feel good.

2. *Do not keep your job hunt a secret:* The only time you should ever keep your job search a secret is if you are still working. (In that case do everything in your power to keep your current company from finding out your intentions.) Keep in mind that of all the sources of job leads, none is more fruitful than your friends and business contacts. If they are not looking around for you, you are wasting one of your most valuable resources. Do not forget to contact former employers—if you left under good circumstances. They could manufacture a good job for you or recommend you to a colleague at another company.

3. *Be wary of blind ads:* If you are still working and looking for a job, I urge you to be very careful about so-called "blind" ads—ads that have a box number but do not reveal the company name. True, some appealing-looking jobs are often advertised in blind ads, but consider the risk. You have no idea

who is getting your response. In the event the person who receives your letter knows your firm or your boss, you could find yourself without a job.

4.   *Keep a lot of things going:* You are only looking for one job, but you improve the odds of getting a good job if you have extra irons in the fire. Whatever you do, do not make the mistake of assuming a particular job is in the bag before you have actually been hired.

PUTTING TOGETHER A WINNING RÉSUMÉ

The résumé is a necessary evil in any job-hunting situation. I say "evil" because nobody is going to hire you on the basis of your résumé alone, but your résumé could easily knock you out of the running, for reasons that may have nothing to do with your qualifications.

The first principle in putting together a résumé is to resist the temptation to have it done by a professional. Our Burke survey shows that the great majority of CPA partners (72.5 per cent), top corporate management (84 per cent), and personnel directors (84 per cent) said that they can detect when a résumé has been prepared professionally. Although most of those interviewed did not feel that a professionally prepared résumé might hurt the chances of a candidate, a substantial minority took the opposite view. Some 10 per cent of CPA partners who said they could detect a professionally prepared résumé also felt that it would hurt a candidate's chances, and about 20 per cent of top management personnel and 18 per cent of personnel directors and managers took the same position.

An even more important reason for doing the résumé yourself is that by doing so you are forced to examine precisely what you have to offer a prospective employer. Developing your own résumé compels you to examine your accomplishments and, therefore, to develop a perspective about yourself that invariably helps you to perform better in the job interview.

As you may know, there are different types of résumés. The most common is the chronological résumé, in which you list your experience from the present backward. Somewhat less common is the functional résumé, in which you organize the résumé according to specific categories of experience and not time. There is also a hybrid form, in which you combine elements of the two.

Generally speaking, you are better off with the chronological résumé. The problem with the functional résumé is that some personnel directors feel that it has been written to conceal something— perhaps the fact that you have had too many jobs.

I am not going to go into the details of how you write the résumé, but I would urge you to look at some of the books on getting jobs. There are a number of such books, including *The Robert Half Way to Get Hired in Today's Job Market,* and nearly all of them include ideas on résumés. However, a few points bear special mention:

1.   *Keep it as brief as possible:* A résumé should never be longer than two pages. The best way to keep it brief is to include only relevant information.

2.   *Stress accomplishments:* Instead of just listing the positions you have held and the responsibilities that were part of those positions, make sure you list what you accomplished in those positions. If you were able to save your firm money through an idea or system you instituted, do not mention only the idea or system; communicate the fact that you saved money as well.

3.   *Keep the tone businesslike:* Except for the final comment on your résumé (if you choose to include a comment), avoid the word "I" and keep the tone straightforward and direct throughout.

4.   *Use active words:* Keep sentences brief and, if possible, start sentences with active verbs: "Developed a system that produced detailed sales analysis."

5.   *Do not mention race or religion:* You should also exclude membership in any organization that might indicate race or religion. These are not relevant. Experience and skill are.

6.   *Be honest:* Under no circumstances should you write anything in the résumé that is not truthful.

7.   *Leave out the following:* Salary requirements (you can talk about them during the interview), references (you can supply them on request), and photograph (no one expects it).

A last word about résumés. I have recommended to many accountants who were looking for jobs that they prepare not one but several different résumés, each truthful but emphasizing a somewhat different aspect of their experience. One of your résumés, for instance, might be for a public accounting position and another for management accounting. One résumé might be tailored to a position as a specialist, another to a position as a generalist. In certain situations, I would even recommend that you tailor a résumé to a specific company, assuming, that is, that you know of a specific job you want at that company.

WHOM TO SEEK OUT

There are several sources of job leads, the most obvious of which are want ads and personnel recruiters, and you should use all of them. However, the most fruitful source of job leads is the one that many accountants looking for a job fail to use to their best advantage: your own contacts. Simply put, a contact is anybody who, directly or indirectly, might produce a job lead for you. It could be a relative, a business associate, or a golf partner. The fact is that nearly everybody you know could be the source of a job lead.

Unfortunately, most accountants looking for a job fail to capitalize on their contacts. The reason, in many cases, is nothing more than pride—foolish pride, I might add. Embarrassed by their situation, uncomfortable about asking for "favors" or "imposing" on friends and acquaintances, many accountants make the most fundamental mistake they can make when they are looking for a job (and I mentioned this before): they keep it a secret.

Do not make the same mistake. In fact, the first thing you should do when you begin to organize your job search is to write down the names of *everybody* you know who even remotely might be able to give you a job lead. Then, divide the list into two groups: those who might be in a position to help you *directly*—perhaps set up an interview for you—and those who might *know* people who could set up an interview for you. Remember, too, that the new people you meet on your search can become useful contacts, provided you make a favorable impression. I can recall any number of occasions when accountants we sent out on job interviews did not get the job we sent them out on, but so impressed the interviewer that they were given additional leads that eventually paid off.

I consider contacts so fundamental to job searching that I recommend to accountants looking for work that they collect as many names as they can in as many places as they can. Once you have started collecting the names, do not be shy about contacting them. As long as you are courteous and direct, the people you contact are not going to be angry with you for seeking their help.

PUBLICATIONS: BEYOND THE OBVIOUS

Naturally, if you are looking for work, you should be following the want ads of local papers, but there are some less obvious media sources for jobs that could yield even better results. For instance, if you are a public accountant, I strongly recommend that you subscribe to the *Public Accounting Report.* This monthly newsletter can give you a great deal of insight into what is going on in the profession and, in the process, provide some valuable job leads. By reading the section of the report that lists client moves from one CPA firm to another, you can get a good sense of where the jobs are in public accounting. Clearly, a firm that is picking up new clients and losing very few is going to need personnel. You will also get some insight into which branches of the large and medium-sized firms are getting the business.

Even if you are a management accountant, you might find the report useful. If you are looking for a controllership position—or its equivalent—you might look at a company switching CPA firms. Why? Because when a company changes CPA firms, there is a fairly good chance it may be in the process of changing its own financial personnel as well. A letter to the president or a high-level officer in which you outline your qualifications is a good idea as well.

Finally, you should pay close attention to the major business publications, such as *The Wall Street Journal, Forbes,* and *Business Week.* Look for signs of anything that could indicate an opportunity for you—a merger or acquisition, an unusually good year, a new CEO.

GETTING THE MOST OUT OF A RECRUITER

My advice when it comes to selecting a personnel recruiter is to visit several of them and let your judgment and instinct decide which of them suits you best. You will probably do best, however, with a service that specializes in accounting and financial positions.

When dealing with recruiters, remember that you are not required to confine your search to one service (although if you are currently employed, it is probably a good idea to limit your search to one or two firms at the most, just to protect yourself). Also, you should be wary of personnel consultants, who, for a fee that can range between $1000 and $10,000 (I heard of one that charged a client $25,000), will guide you with your résumé and job search. If you elect to go that route, make sure you check the firm's references and contact the Better Business Bureau to find out if there have been any significant complaints.

HANDLING THE JOB INTERVIEW

The job interview, as you probably know, is the single most important aspect of a job-hunting campaign. No matter how organized you are or how diligent you are about tracking down job leads, if you do not sell yourself in the job interview, your chances of getting the job you want are remote.

The best way to approach a job interview is to think of it as a kind of stage audition—a performance. You've been given a chance to "read" for a part, and it is up to you to perform in a way that will convince the interviewer that you are the person to hire.

DOING YOUR HOMEWORK

One of the cardinal rules of successful interviewing is never to go into an interview without being totally prepared for it. Go into the interview knowing as much about the organization interviewing you as you can. If it is a public accounting firm, you should know how big the firm is and what kind of clients it has. If it is a corporation, you should know its products, its size, and, if possible, its recent earnings. It would help, too, to know something about the company's strengths and weaknesses.

You can get this information from a variety of sources. Business directories—*Moody's, Dun & Bradstreet's, Standard & Poor's*—will give the basic information on larger companies, and you might also be able to find references to articles about these companies in *Reader's Guide to Periodical Literature.* As far as smaller companies are concerned, you will have to be more resourceful. Your bank may be willing to get a Dun & Bradstreet report on a company for you. It would give you interesting historical background along with financial information. Try to talk to people who may know of the company. Better still, try to find an accountant who has worked for the firm in which you are interested.

I would strongly recommend, too, that you do what you can to find out about the person interviewing you. Here, again, library sources such as *Who's Who* might help, but you will probably have to get the information from the people who recommended you for the interview. What sort of information should you look for? The type of personality —whether the person interviewing is aggressive, for instance—would be good to know, but just as useful is information about the person's interests.

Getting this information is not always easy. It may take some digging—but it is extremely helpful. One of our Burke surveys showed that 75 per cent of interviewers feel that not being familiar with their company hurts your chances of getting hired.

PREPARING FOR THE QUESTIONS

No two job interviews are exactly the same, but you can count on certain questions being asked. You can be sure, for instance, that the interviewer is going to ask you to talk a little about yourself and to give the reasons you can handle the job. If you are still working, you will be asked why you want to leave your present job. From most interviewers, you can expect a question about your long-range goals, and a favorite question these days is what your weaknesses are.

There is no pat way to answer these questions, although there are some guidelines to bear in mind:

1. *Be honest:* I cannot think of any good reasons that would justify lying in a job interview, and I can think of a lot of reasons you should not. The most obvious is that if an interviewer even remotely suspects you are lying, your chances of getting hired are nil. What do you do if asked a question that might not show you off in the best light? Answer the question quickly and move on to some other, more positive aspect of yourself. For instance, the interviewer says to you, "But you have no experience in the publishing industry, do you?" Your answer might be, "That's true, but I've worked for clients in the music industry and I think that there are some similarities." (Assuming, that is, that you actually had music industry clients.)

2. *Be a good listener:* Concentrate on what the interviewer is saying to you, and be responsive. Nod when you are in agreement. Smile when it is appropriate to smile. Stay actively involved in the conversation.

3. *Be careful of your body language:* More interviewers than you might think will be judging you on how you sit (be relaxed but do not slouch) and on whether you look them in the eye when you speak to them.

4. *Keep your cool:* On rare occasions, you might run into an interviewer who seems to be doing everything possible to get you angry. On the outside chance that the interviewer is simply testing your ability to deal with pressure, keep your cool at all costs.

5. *Brush up on your accounting:* Brush up particularly on the technical aspects of your specialty. You can be sure that your technical background will be discussed during the interview, but tailor the complexity of your response to the background of the interviewer. If you are talking to someone in personnel, for instance, make sure you avoid technical jargon.

One of the best ways I know of to prepare for the questions you are likely to be asked in a job interview is to practice answering questions in front of a mirror. Here are five questions of the many you might work with:

1.   What are your long-term career goals?

2.   Why do you want to work for our firm?

3.   What can you offer this company?

4.   Where do you see yourself in five years?

5.   What courses did you like best and least in school?

Practice answering these questions into a tape recorder while you sit in front of a mirror. As you do so, try to notice whether your answers appear thoughtful. Check for disturbing mannerisms or lack of eye contact—anything that could distract an interviewer.

ANSWERING DIFFICULT QUESTIONS

The better the interviewer, the more probing and difficult the questions you are asked are likely to be. Good interviewers will look for obvious gaps in your credentials and your background and will press you to defend whatever they feel might be a weakness in your experience.

What you say in answer to these questions probably is not as important as *how* you say it. If you become visibly upset or overly defensive, you are communicating a message about your ability to handle stress, forgetting how you answer the question. If, on the other hand, you deal forthrightly with these difficult questions, you can win points in the other direction.

One excellent technique to use when you find yourself on the defensive is to concede at least part of the point the interviewer is asking but to counterattack with a logical explanation. If the interviewer suggests, for example, that your résumé does not reveal any direct experience in a particular aspect of the job for which you are being interviewed—supervisory skills—your answer might well be, "It's true, I didn't have any specific managerial duties in my last job, but I worked on several specific outside projects in which I was responsible for the work of other people." This practice—that of conceding first before you defend—will almost always work better than an answer that does not acknowledge the validity of the questioner's concern. One of the worst things you can do during a job interview is to tell the interviewer what he or she should or should not "worry about." You need to accept any question you get during an interview as a reflection of some concern, and regardless of how you answer the question, you need to make sure you alleviate that concern.

WHAT TO AVOID

In one of the Burke surveys we conducted a few years ago, we asked personnel directors to identify the most common mistakes made by candidates. Here is a brief summary of the findings:

1. *Poor grooming and inappropriate dress:* Interviewers, as we have already established, place great importance on how you look. They want someone, above all, who looks businesslike and professional.

2. *Lack of enthusiasm:* You are better off being *too* enthusiastic than being withdrawn or indifferent.

3. *Failure to ask questions about the job:* Interviewers like to see you reflect a serious interest in the duties and responsibilities of the job.

4. *Asking direct questions about salaries and fringes too early in the interview:* Save these questions until the offer is made.

5. *Desperation:* Despair may gain you sympathy, but it will not get you hired. In fact, showing desperation is almost guaranteed to lose you the offer.

6. *Exaggerating skills or accomplishments:* Interviewers can usually tell when you are stretching the truth and will almost invariably consider it a strike against you.

7. *Not knowing enough about the company:* Interviewers like to see that you are interested in the company (as opposed to a job for the sake of a job).

8. *Not maintaining eye contact:* Many interviewers perceive (rightly or wrongly) that if you fail to look them in the eye, you are trying to hide something.

9. *Showing a lack of confidence:* Interviewers expect you to be a little nervous at an interview, but there is a difference between being a little nervous and showing a lack of confidence. All things being equal, interviewers would prefer to see you overconfident rather than underconfident.

SHOULD YOU TAKE THE OFFER?

Not getting an offer after a job interview can be depressing, but being offered—and taking—the wrong job can be much worse. Not only can it lock you into an unhappy situation, but it can also set your career plans back for years. "It can be a tough situation," says Kenneth S. Asch, our Long Island office franchisee. "A lot of accountants are very flattered when the first offer comes in—particularly if the money is good. But what they don't do is consider the job within the framework of an overall career plan."

Do not misunderstand me. Career planning is an academic point if you have been out of work for several months, but, with most accountants, the situation is not that critical. Kenneth Asch told me of one young public accountant, for instance, who had been making $32,000 and wanted to move into private accounting. She had two offers. One was for an industrial company and paid $38,000. The other was to take over the branch office of a bank and paid $40,000. The accountant chose the bank job only because it paid more money, not realizing that the career potential in the other job was far greater.

Another mistake many accountants make when it comes to a job offer is to concern themselves too much with the job and not enough with the firm or company. There are exceptions, I grant you, but for the most part the better the firm you join, the better your career interests will be served. Notice that I did not say "bigger," for size is not the issue. Quality is. "All things considered," says Alex Cohen of *The Practical Accountant,*

> you should look for a firm that's going to help you get ahead, a firm with a good reputation and expertise and management who are respected and knowledgeable. You want a firm of high quality standards that brings people along, that has a liberal partnership program and esprit de corps.

But how do you decide how good a firm is before you work for it? There are any number of barometers you can use, but here, to my mind, are hallmarks of quality firms in public accounting and in industry at large.

1.   They are in a growth pattern
2.   They enjoy an excellent reputation with other firms
3.   They do not have *excessive* turnover
4.   They encourage employees to get involved with professional societies (to the point of paying the dues)
5.   They put part of their earnings back into the firm
6.   They are headed by a management team rather than by one person
7.   They have a reasonably rapid rate of advancement

Let me point out that some of the firms that meet these criteria might not necessarily be right for you, depending on your career expectations and depending, too, on whether you are in public accounting or management accounting. In public accounting, for instance, you should never join a firm unless you fully understand—and support—the company's partnership philosophy and policy. The better firms will be honest with you when you question them about their partnership policy. You can get a general idea of how quickly they tend to promote to partner and what kind of financial obligations would accrue if you were to become a partner. You should also be able to get an idea of what qualities the firm is looking for in a partner.

It is difficult to set up any sort of evaluative scale on the various partnership policies in public accounting. In the end, it is a matter of which policy suits you best. The point to bear in mind here is that you should find out as much as you can about these policies and other policies before you join any firm. After all, you are making one of the biggest and most important decisions of your life. It is a decision that deserves all the time you can give it.

CONCLUSION

_____

Success takes just a little
more work than failure.

What I have tried to do in this book is to share with you some of what I have observed and learned over the past 35 years about career success in accounting and what some of today's most successful accountants and business people have to say about the subject. As you realize by now, neither I nor any of the people I interviewed for this book offered you any magic formulas to achieve career success, and we did not offer any short cuts, either. As I mentioned at the start of Chapter Two, the only easy way to success is to work hard.

On the other hand, the amount of work embodied in most of the advice found throughout this book is not as much as you might think, not if you are truly dedicated to achieving career success and not if you begin to implement this advice in systematic fashion. How much extra time would it take you, for instance, to look as good as you are capable of looking each day when you go to work? How much harder would you have to work to establish yourself as one of the main contributors in your firm? And, how deep an intrusion into your personal life would there be if you spent two or three nights a month to become active in a professional group, or if you were to give speeches to local groups once every six weeks or so or write two or three articles a year worthy of publication?

No, time is not the obstacle. The obstacle is commitment: making up your mind that you _want_ to get the most you can out of your career, that you are worthy and deserving of this success, and, finally, that whatever small sacrifices you may have to make will more than pay for themselves in the long run. The mere fact that you are an accountant indicates that you already have the basic tools for success. How far these tools will take you is entirely up to you.

Let me make one final point. It is one thing to be motivated by success and quite another thing to be obsessed by it. The difference is crucial because the more obsessed you are with success, the less you will be able to enjoy it once you have achieved it and the more damage you are likely to do not only to yourself but to the people close to you.

I can not tell you how to live your life, nor I can set your priorities for you, but I can at least offer a small suggestion that could go a very long way to enrich your life—regardless of how busy you are, try to set aside at least a few hours once a month and use this time to take what I would call an inventory of your life.

Start with thinking about your health. Are you feeling as good as you should? Do you maintain a reasonably healthy lifestyle, that is, getting enough exercise, watching your weight, eating a good diet? Or, on the other hand, is there a chance that your desire to get ahead is having an *adverse* effect on your health—so much so that if you continue at your present pace, you may not be healthy enough to appreciate whatever success you attain.

Take time, too, to think about the quality of your personal relationships. Time is a precious commodity to anybody on a success track, but if so much of your time is wrapped up in your career that there is no quality time left for your family or close friends, the equation is eventually going to catch up to you. I have been extraordinarily fortunate in my own life to have had not only an interesting and exciting career but a rich family life as well, and I cannot imagine how my life might have been if I had been unable to share my success with my wife, my children, and, now, my grandchildren.

Finally, ask yourself one simple question: are you enjoying yourself? As I pointed out early in the book, one of the things that nearly all highly successful people have in common is that they genuinely enjoy what they do. Yes, the goals they set for themselves are important, but so, too, are the paths they take en route to these goals. Follow their example. Strive for success, but make sure you enjoy the ride, too.

On the following pages are highlights from the Accountant Attitude Study conducted by Burke Marketing Research for Robert Half International Inc. The purpose of the study was to determine attitudes among various executives, both in and out of accounting, with regard to the accounting profession.

Appendix Table A. Highlights from Burke Accountant Attitude Study

Survey statements	Responses, %, from			
	Chief financial officers	CPA partners	Top corporate management	Corporate personnel directors
Would choose accounting as profession again				
Agree strongly	66.7	68.6	28.0	
Agree somewhat	13.7	21.6	46.0	
Neither agree nor disagree	2.0	2.0	16.0	
Disagree somewhat	9.5	3.9	8.0	
Disagree strongly	5.9	3.9	—	
Don't know	2.0	—	2.0	

Appendix Table A (*continued*). Highlights from Burke Accountant Attitude Study

Survey statements	Responses, %, from			
	Chief financial officers	CPA partners	Top corporate management	Corporate personnel directors
Opportunities in today's business climate better than ever for accountants				
Agree strongly	64.7	54.9	30.0	34.0
Agree somewhat	27.5	37.3	50.0	52.0
Neither agree nor disagree	5.9	3.9	8.0	6.0
Disagree somewhat	2.0	2.0	12.0	6.0
Disagree strongly	—	2.0	—	2.0
Accounting is an excellent field for *men* looking to advance quickly				
Agree strongly	35.3	37.3	16.0	10.0
Agree somewhat	35.3	49.0	42.8	34.0
Neither agree nor disagree	9.8	—	26.0	26.0
Disagree somewhat	15.7	11.8	12.0	16.0
Disagree strongly	2.0	2.0	2.0	12.0
Don't know	2.0	—	2.0	2.0
Accounting is an excellent field for *women* looking to advance quickly				
Agree strongly	62.7	47.1	34.0	26.0
Agree somewhat	29.4	33.3	50.0	36.0
Accounting is an excellent field for *women* looking to advance quickly				
Neither agree nor disagree	2.0	7.8	10.0	16.0
Disagree somewhat	3.9	5.9	4.0	14.0
Disagree strongly	—	3.9	2.0	6.0
Don't know	2.0	2.0	—	2.0
Accountants are entrepreneurial in their thinking				
Agree strongly	5.9	25.5		
Agree somewhat	31.4	41.2		
Neither agree nor disagree	11.5	5.9		
Disagree somewhat	37.3	13.7		
Disagree strongly	11.8	5.9		
Don't know	2.0	7.8		

Appendix Table A (*continued*). Highlights from Burke Accountant Attitude Study

	Responses, %, from			
Survey statements	Chief financial officers	CPA partners	Top corporate management	Corporate personnel directors
Public accountants lack education and training in economics				
Agree strongly	5.9	5.9		
Agree somewhat	31.4	17.6		
Neither agree nor disagree	9.8	11.8		
Disagree somewhat	43.1	39.2		
Disagree strongly	5.9	25.5		
Don't know	3.9	—		
Public accountants lack education and training in budgets				
Agree strongly	7.8	3.9		
Agree somewhat	35.3	23.5		
Neither agree nor disagree	3.9	7.8		
Disagree somewhat	35.3	41.2		
Disagree strongly	15.7	23.5		
Don't know	2.0	—		
Public acccounts lack education and training in cost accounting				
Agree strongly	9.8	11.8		
Agree somewhat	29.4	23.5		
Neither agree nor disagree	5.9	7.8		
Disagree somewhat	35.3	31.4		
Disagree strongly	17.6	23.5		
Don't know	2.0	2.0		
Accountant with MBA more likely to get ahead than one without MBA				
Agree strongly	33.3	31.4	50.0	38.0
Agree somewhat	39.2	27.5	32.0	46.0
Neither agree nor disagree	9.8	13.7	6.0	4.0
Accountant with MBA more likely to get ahead than one without MBA				
Disagree somewhat	9.8	17.6	4.0	8.0
Disagree strongly	5.9	9.8	4.0	4.0
Don't know	2.0	—	4.0	—

Appendix Table A (*continued*). Highlights from Burke Accountant Attitude Study

	Responses, %, from			
Survey statements	Chief financial officers	CPA partners	Top corporate management	Corporate personnel directors
Accountant undervalued/underpaid in public accounting				
Agree strongly	—	21.6		
Agree somewhat	13.7	19.6		
Neither agree nor disagree	13.7	11.8		
Disagree somewhat	43.1	39.2		
Disagree strongly	21.6	7.8		
Don't know	7.8	—		
Accountants undervalued/underpaid in management accounting				
Agree strongly	7.8	7.8	4.0	6.0
Agree somewhat	19.6	11.8	14.0	16 0
Neither agree nor disagree	21.6	23.5	26.0	8.0
Disagree somewhat	37.3	41.2	44.0	46.0
Disagree strongly	11.8	5.9	8.0	20.0
Don't know	2.0	9.8	4.0	4.0
Easier for articulate accountants to get ahead in public accounting				
Agree strongly	72.5	78.4		
Agree somewhat	21.6	17.6		
Neither agree nor disagree	2.0	2.0		
Disagree somewhat	2.0	2.0		
Disagree strongly	—	—		
Don't know	2.0	—		
Easier for articulate acccountants to get ahead in management accounting				
Agree strongly	72.5	62.7	60.0	66.0
Agree somewhat	27.5	21.6	38.0	34.0
Neither agree nor disagree	—	9.8	—	—
Disagree somewhat	—	3.9	2.0	—
Disagree strongly	—	—	—	—
Don't know	—	2.0	—	—

Appendix Table A (*continued*). Highlights from Burke Accountant Attitude Study

Survey statements	Chief financial officers	CPA partners	Top corporate management	Corporate personnel directors
	Responses, %, from			

Accountants in business for themselves are usually successful

Agree strongly	—	19.6	—	6.0
Agree somewhat	25.5	52.9	24.0	24.0
Neither agree nor disagree	31.4	13.7	44.0	40.0
Disagree somewhat	25.5	7.8	14.0	14.0

Accountants in business for themselves are usually successful

Disagree strongly	2.0	—	4.0	2.0
Don't know	15.7	5.9	14.0	14.0

Importance of being a CPA in public accounting

Very important	92.2	98.0		
Somewhat important	5.9	2.0		
Neither important nor unimportant	—	—		
Somewhat unimportant	—	—		
Very unimportant	—	—		
Don't know	2.0	—		

Importance of being a CPA in management accounting

Very important	11.8	29.4	32.0	30.0
Somewhat important	62.7	58.8	56.0	50.0
Neither important nor unimportant	11.8	—	2.0	4.0
Somewhat unimportant	9.8	5.9	8.0	12.0
Very important	3.9	—	—	4.0
Don't know	—	5.9	2.0	—

Appendix Table A (*continued*). Highlights from Burke Accountant Attitude Study

	Responses, %, from			
Survey statements	Chief financial officers	CPA partners	Top corporate management	Corporate personnel directors
Importance of having knowledge of computers in public accounting				
Very important	62.7	45.1		
Somewhat important	33.3	52.9		
Neither important nor unimportant	3.9	2.0		
Somewhat unimportant	—	—		
Very unimportant	—	—		
Don't know	—	—		
Importance of having knowledge of computers in management accounting				
Very important	66.7	72.5	70.0	74.0
Somewhat important	33.3	21.6	24.0	24.0
Neither important nor unimportant	—	2.0	6.0	—
Somewhat unimportant	—	2.0	—	2.0
Very unimportant	—	—	—	—
Don't know	—	2.0	—	—
Importance of specializing within public accounting				
Very important	23.5	33.3		
Somewhat important	41.2	35.3		
Importance of specializing within public accounting				
Neither important nor unimportant	9.8	13.7		
Somewhat unimportant	11.8	15.7		
Very unimportant	2.0	2.0		
Don't know	11.8	—		

Appendix Table A (*continued*). Highlights from Burke Accountant Attitude Study

Survey statements	Responses, %, from			
	Chief financial officers	CPA partners	Top corporate management	Corporate personnel directors
Importance of specializing within management accouting				
Very important	2.0	13.7		
Somewhat important	31.4	33.3		
Neither important nor unimportant	11.8	19.6		
Somewhat unimportant	33.3	23.5		
Very unimportant	15.7	3.9		
Don't know	5.9	5.9		
Importance of belonging to a trade association				
Very important	2.0	13.7		
Somewhat important	43.1	43.1		
Neither important nor unimportant	13.7	9.8		
Somewhat unimportant	25.5	25.5		
Very unimportant	11.8	5.9		
Don't know	3.9	2.0		
Importance of having articles published				
Very important	2.0	3.9		
Somewhat important	21.6	33.3		
Neither important nor unimportant	25.5	11.8		
Somewhat unimportant	29.4	35.3		
Very unimportant	19.6	15.7		
Don't know	2.0	—		

Appendix Table A (*continued*). Highlights from Burke Accountant Attitude Study

	Responses, %, from			
Survey statements	Chief financial officers	CPA partners	Top corporate management	Corporate personnel directors
Importance of assisting in public service				
Very important	5.9	25.5		
Somewhat important	45.1	47.1		
Neither important nor unimportant	19.6	11.8		
Somewhat unimportant	21.6	9.8		
Very unimportant	5.9	3.9		
Don't know	2.0	2.0		
Importance of CMA				
Very important	2.0	2.0		
Somewhat important	31.4	31.4		
Neither important nor unimportant	15.7	7.8		
Somewhat unimportant	25.5	5.9		
Very unimportant	9.8	2.0		
Don't know	—	7.8		
Not aware of CMA	15.7	43.1	62.0	58.0
Public accountants have ability to get along well with people				
Agree strongly	15.7	41.2	10.0	14.0
Agree somewhat	54.9	43.1	46.0	46.0
Neither agree nor disagree	19.6	5.9	26.0	25.0
Disagree somewhat	5.9	5.9	16.0	6.0
Disagree strongly	—	—	—	2.0
Don't know	3.9	3.9	2.0	4.0

Appendix Table A (*continued*). Highlights from Burke Accountant Attitude Study

	Responses, %, from			
Survey statements	Chief financial officers	CPA partners	Top corporate management	Corporate personnel directors
Public accountants have good communication skills				
Agree strongly	17.6	45.1	6.0	14.0
Agree somewhat	54.9	39.2	46.0	50.0
Neither agree nor disagree	17.6	5.9	22.0	18.0
Disagree somewhat	9.8	5.9	26.0	10.0
Disagree strongly	—	2.0	—	2.0
Don't know	—	2.0	—	6.0
Public accountants have a high level of technical skills				
Agree strongly	49.0	37.3	24.0	30.0
Agree somewhat	45.1	51.0	34.0	48.0
Neither agree nor disagree	5.9	2.0	22.0	14.0
Disagree somewhat	—	7.8	16.0	6.0
Disagree strongly	—	—	—	—
Don't know	—	2.0	4.0	2.0
Public accountants are highly intelligent				
Agree strongly	23.5	27.5	8.0	8.0
Agree somewhat	49.0	54.9	42.0	48.0
Neither agree nor disagree	19.5	13.7	36.0	30.0
Disagree somewhat	2.0	2.0	8.0	8.0
Disagree strongly	—	—	2.0	—
Don't know	5.9	2.0	4.0	6.0
Public accountants are well-rounded business persons				
Agree strongly	—	21.6	—	6.0
Agree somewhat	37.3	35.3	26.0	32.0
Neither agree nor disagree	15.7	17.6	28.0	16.0
Disagree somewhat	37.3	23.5	38.0	34.0
Disagree strongly	5.9	—	4.0	8.0
Don't know	3.9	2.0	4.0	4.0

Appendix Table A (*continued*). Highlights from Burke Accountant Attitude Study

Survey statements	Responses, %, from			
	Chief financial officers	CPA partners	Top corporate management	Corporate personnel directors
Management accountants are able to get along well with people				
Agree strongly	9.8	7.8	6.0	10.0
Agree somewhat	62.7	56.9	46.0	56.0
Neither agree nor disagree	21.6	17.6	30.0	22.0
Disagree somewhat	5.9	11.8	14.0	12.0
Disagree strongly	—	2.0	2.0	—
Don't know	—	3.9	2.0	—
Management accountants have good communication skills				
Agree strongly	15.7	19.6	8.0	12.0
Agree somewhat	39.2	47.1	42.0	54.0
Neither agree nor disagree	29.4	15.7	18.0	20.0
Disagree somewhat	13.7	13.7	30.0	14.0
Disagree strongly	—	2.0	—	—
Don't know	2.0	2.0	2.0	—
Management accountants have a high level of technical skills				
Agree strongly	15.7	13.7	14.0	18.0
Agree somewhat	68.6	58.8	48.0	60.0
Neither agree nor disagree	9.8	11.8	24.0	12.0
Disagree somewhat	3.9	11.8	12.0	10.0
Disagree strongly	—	—	—	—
Don't know	2.0	3.9	2.0	—
Management accountants are highly intelligent				
Agree strongly	11.8	13.7	8.0	8.0
Agree somewhat	58.8	62.7	42.0	58.0
Neither agree nor disagree	25.5	13.7	36.0	30.0
Disagree somewhat	2.0	5.9	10.0	2.0
Disagree strongly	—	—	2.0	—
Don't know	2.0	3.9	2.0	2.0

Appendix Table A (*continued*). Highlights from Burke Accountant Attitude Study

Survey statements	Responses, %, from			
	Chief financial officers	CPA partners	Top corporate management	Corporate personnel directors
Management accountants are well-rounded business persons				
Agree strongly	7.8	7.8	—	6.0
Agree somewhat	41.2	41.2	38.0	52.0
Neither agree nor disagree	27.5	15.7	24.0	14.0
Disagree somewhat	15.7	29.4	30.0	24.0
Disagree strongly	2.0	2.0	4.0	4.0
Don't know	5.9	3.9	4.0	—
Chief executivee officer has strong accounting or finance background				
Yes	33.3	—	38.0	30.0
No	66.7	—	60.0	68.0
Don't know	—	—	2.0	2.0
Accountants are too numbers oriented				
Agree strongly	13.7	18.0		
Agree somewhat	54.9	52.0		
Neither agree nor disagree	7.8	8.0		
Disagree somewhat	13.7	18.0		
Disagree strongly	3.9	4.0		
Don't know	5.9	—		
Accountants lack imagination				
Agree strongly	3.9	14.0		
Agree somewhat	23.5	42.0		
Neither agree nor disagree	9.8	12.0		
Disagree somewhat	41.2	30.0		
Disagree strongly	17.6	2.0		
Don't know	3.9	—		

Appendix Table A (*continued*). Highlights from Burke Accountant Attitude Study

Survey statements	Chief financial officers	CPA partners	Top corporate management	Corporate personnel directors
	Responses, %, from			
Accountants are poor listeners				
Agree strongly	2.0	2.0		
Agree somewhat	17.6	16.0		
Neither agree nor disagree	—	30.0		
Disagree somewhat	45.1	42.0		
Disagree strongly	33.3	8.0		
Don't know	2.0	2.0		
Accountants are poor communicators				
Agree strongly	2.0	4.0		
Agree somewhat	19.6	38.0		
Neither agree nor disagree	3.9	22.0		
Disagree somewhat	43.1	30.0		
Accountants are poor communicators				
Disagree strongly		29.4	6.0	
Don't know		2.0	—	
Accountants are too conservative				
Agree strongly		7.8	8.0	
Agree somewhat		49.0	46.0	
Neither agree nor disagree		13.7	30.0	
Disagree somewhat		25.5	14.0	
Disagree strongly		2.0	2.0	
Don't know		2.0	—	

Appendix Table A (*continued*). Highlights from Burke Accountant Attitude Study

	Responses, %, from			
Survey statements	Chief financial officers	CPA partners	Top corporate management	Corporate personnel directors
Accountants are not good decision makers				
Agree strongly		—	8.0	
Agree somewhat		13.7	24.0	
Neither agree nor disagree		3.9	28.0	
Disagree somewhat		52.9	40.0	
Disagree strongly		27.5	—	
Don't know		2.0	—	
Acccountants are weak in managerial skills				
Agree strongly		3.9	6.0	
Agree somewhat		33.3	44.0	
Neither agree nor disagree		9.8	22.0	
Disagree somewhat		39.2	24.0	
Disagree strongly		11.8	2.0	
Don't know		2.0	2.0	

Appendix Table B. Queries from Burke Accountant Attitude Study

	Responses, %, from	
Survery questions	Chief financial officers	CPA partners
What single piece of advice would you give to accountants just starting out in public accounting[a]		
Career path		
Get as much experience or as varied experience as possible	13.7	21.6

Appendix Table B (*continued*). Queries from Burke Accountant Attitude Study

Survery questions	Responses, %, from	
	Chief financial officers	CPA partners
What single piece of advice would you give to accountants just starting out in public accounting[a]		
Go with a big, a national, an established, or a growing firm	9.8	15.7
Do not specialize	5.9	5.9
Join a medium-sized, local firm	—	5.9
Specialize	—	3.9
Miscellaneous career path	9.8	5.9
Education and communications skills		
Learn and get as much education as possible	9.8	23.5
Pass the examination for the CPA examination and get your certificate	11.8	7.8
Improve communication skills	5.9	3.9
Miscellaneous education and communication skills	2.0	—
Personal attitudes		
Work hard and long hours	15.7	15.7
Persist. Stay with it for at least 5 years	5.9	9.8
Use common sense	5.9	2.0
Be patient and go slow	—	5.9
Miscellaneous personal attitudes	7.8	—
Miscellaneous		
Explore other fields	5.9	2.0
Other miscellaneous	—	2.0
Don't know or none	11.8	3.9

Appendix Table B (*continued*). Queries from Burke Accountant Attitude Study

	Responses, %, from	
	Chief financial officers	CPA partners
Survery questions		
What single piece of advice would you give to accountants just starting out in management accounting[a]		
Education and communications skills		
Learn all you can about the business, company, or firm	25.5	7.8
Get CPA certificate	3.9	7.8
Get as much education as possible	3.9	5.9
Develop communication skills	7.8	2.0
Pass CMA examination or join CMA programs	3.9	2.0
Get a master's degree	3.9	2.0
Get into a management training program	2.0	2.0
Learn about data processing, systems, computer field	3.9	—
Stay abreast of current developments in the profession	2.0	—
Get the management certificate	2.0	—
Miscellaneous education and communication skills	5.9	2.0
Personal attitudes		
Work hard, long hours, be conscientious	17.6	3.9
Get involved, be aggressive, visible, open	7.3	2.0
Be creative and innovative	2.0	3.9
Use common sense	2.0	2.0
Miscellaneous personal attitudes	2.0	5.9
Career path		
Get into public accounting first	2.0	11.8
Get as much experience and as varied experience as possible	7.8	2.0
Miscellaneous career path	7.8	3.9
Miscellaneous		
Other miscellaneous	—	5.9
Don't know or none	3.9	37.3

Appendix Table B (*continued*). Queries from Burke Accountant Attitude Study

	Responses, %, from	
Survery questions	Chief financial officers	CPA partners

What single piece of advice would you give to accountants who are thinking of going into business for themselves?[a]

	Chief financial officers	CPA partners
Career paths		
Get as much experience and as varied experience as possible	13.7	7.8
Have a good client base and develop clientele	7.8	7.8
Work for a large firm first	3.9	7.8
Be responsive to client's needs and give them individual attention	3.9	5.9
Be well organized; keep good records, accounts, tax systems	2.0	3.9
Get a good partner	2.0	2.0
Set goals for yourself	2.0	2.0
Miscellaneous career paths	3.9	2.0
Personal attitudes		
Be prepared to work hard and keep long hours	7.8	11.8
Be patient and stick with it	—	5.9
Meet people and get involved in community activities	2.0	3.9
Miscellaneous personal attitudes	5.9	2.0
Education and communication skills		
Develop technical competence	2.0	7.8
Develop good communication skills	3.9	—
Specialize	2.0	2.0
Do a lot of research; know the field	—	3.9
Certification is important	2.0	2.0
Miscellaneous education	2.0	—

Appendix Table B (*continued*). Queries from Burke Accountant Attitude Study

Survery questions	Responses, %, from	
	Chief financial officers	CPA partners
What single piece of advice would you give to accountants who are thinking of going into business for themselves[a]		
Miscellaneous		
Have enough working capitol	21.6	11.8
I wouldn't recommend it	9.8	7.8
Weigh the advantages and disadvantages	3.9	—
Do it; the rewards are gratifying	—	3.9
Other miscellaneous	—	2.0
Don't know	21.6	15.7
What single piece of advice would you give management accountants who are thinking of going into public accounting?[a]		
Career paths		
Work for a firm; work for a large firm	3.9	7.8
Do it early in your career	5.9	3.9
Specialize	3.9	2.0
It's better to go from public to management accounting	5.9	—
Develop business contacts	—	2.0
Get as much experience as possible	—	2.0
Miscellaneous career paths	5.9	13.7
Education		
Get a CPA certificate	13.7	9.8
Further education, review, brushup	7.8	11.8
Miscellaneous education	2.0	—

Appendix Table B (*continued*). Queries from Burke Accountant Attitude Study

Survery questions	Responses, %, from	
	Chief financial officers	CPA partners

What single piece of advice would you give management accountants who are thinking of going into public accounting?[a]

Personal attitudes		
Be prepared to work hard and keep long hours	7.8	11.8
You have to be flexible and adaptable to pressure and changes	2.0	9.8
Personal relationships are more important in public accounting	7.8	—
Stick with it; it takes a long time	2.0	2.0
Get active in civic activities	2.0	—
Miscellaneous personal attitudes	3.9	2.0
Miscellaneous		
They are totally different	3.9	13.7
Don't do it	9.8	3.9
Limited earnings in the beginning	3.9	3.9
Can make more money in management accounting	2.0	—
Other miscellaneous	5.9	—
Don't know or none	17.6	23.5

What single piece of advice would you give public accountants who are thinking of going into management accounting[a]

Career path		
Know the type of business; learn about all aspects of the organization	17.6	3.9
Look for the opportunity for advancement	9.8	7.8
Know the firm's financial stability and prospects for future growth	5.9	5.9
Do some research; be sure of the field before going into it	—	7.8
Do not specialize; test different fields	3.9	—
Enter at a high level	2.0	—

Appendix Table B (*continued*). Queries from Burke Accountant Attitude Study

	Responses, %, from	
Survery questions	Chief financial officers	CPA partners

What single piece of advice would you give public accountants who are thinking of going into management accounting[a]

	Chief financial officers	CPA partners
Specialize	—	2.0
Miscellaneous career paths	7.8	—
Education and communication skills		
Learn to communicate with management and associates	5.9	3.9
Brush up on cost systems and cost accounting skills	3.9	2.0
Get CMA; enroll in a CMA program	3.9	—
Be fully qualified	3.9	—
Pursue an MBA	—	2.0
Understand computer analysis	—	2.0
Personal attitudes		
Use initiative and capabilities; demonstrate your skills	5.9	3.9
Work and study hard	2.0	2.0
Don't be too forceful	2.0	—
Miscellaneous personal attitudes	5.9	3.9
Miscellaneous		
Don't go into management; too routine; repetitious; less freedom	2.0	9.8
Do it; it's a good move	5.9	3.9
Be prepared to accept lower salary	2.0	—
Performance requirements are not as strict in public accounting	2.0	—
Other miscellaneous	5.9	2.0
Don't know	11.8	43.1

[a]Percentages do not add up to 100 per cent because some respondents gave more than one answer.

Index